LUTHER'S PROTEST

From 95 Theses to Reformation

JOHN A. BRAUN

NORTHWESTERN PUBLISHING HOUSE
Milwaukee, Wisconsin

Second printing, 2017

Art Director: Karen Knutson
Design Team: Diane Cook, Pamela Dunn, Lynda Williams

Northwestern Publishing House
1250 N. 113th St., Milwaukee, WI 53226-3284
www.nph.net

Published 2016
Printed in the United States of America
ISBN 978-0-8100-2717-6
ISBN 978-0-8100-2718-3 (e-book)

CONTENTS

For Sandy, my Katherine von Bora,

Jenny, Don, Katie, Josh,

Allison, Lucas, Connor, Madelyn, Micah, and Charlotte

PREFACE

Some suffer from historical amnesia. The past is past. Today is today. They look forward to tomorrow, but when tomorrow comes, they cannot remember yesterday accurately. If we find history interesting at all, we organize it into dates and short quotes that help us navigate its complexities. But no history is as tidy and neat as a list of dates or a few memorable quotes make it appear. Neither is it all black and white.

Perhaps the study of church history suffers from an even more severe case of amnesia. We don't know denominational lines. They seem to get in the way of our sense that everyone believes the same thing. But they don't really. Even the scant outline of church history with dates and bullet points we may have learned in some classroom reveals a different reality. A different view begins to dawn in our reflections: the church on earth had more than one controversy over its long history. Protests and differences have led to tragic events, splits, trouble, and even armed conflict.

And so we become curious. We read about the past, and we listen to those who have read more than we have. But whenever we take on the task of reading history, we should first recognize that the writer of the history might be telling a version favorable to one side at the expense of the other. Revision of history is an Olympic event involving finger-pointing and selection of favorable facts while excluding the unfavorable. Church history is no exception, and Reformation history, in particular, perpetuates differing perspectives. Views of Luther and the Reformation diverge along the fault lines of conviction—Lutheran, Roman Catholic, Reformed—and spread even beyond to politics, economics, and philosophy, among other orientations.

This effort to add another history follows the fault line of the Lutheran perspective. However, I hope it remains objective enough not to qualify as propaganda or revision. I simply want to understand my own heritage as a Lutheran Christian and confess why I believe it to be valuable. Together with Roman Catholics and Eastern Orthodox believers, I share the history of the ancient Christian church we have in common. Yet I also conclude that over time the church became dramatically different from the primitive church of the apostles. Some of that development has been helpful and need not be discarded. For example, the rich traditions of worship that we practice into our own age are different from the church of the apostles. But a struggle for supremacy and even an understandable struggle for uniformity contributed to an erosion of the message of the apostolic church. The teachings of the church at the time of the Reformation had assumed a size and shape unrecognizable when compared with the New Testament record. In my view the Reformation was a protest against a church that had strayed from its origins. It was no less a desire to reform it and return it to its foundation—Jesus Christ. ❦

NORTH SEA
BALTIC SEA
Lutterworth
England
London
ENGLISH CHANNEL
HOLY ROMAN EMPIRE
Netherlands
Wittenberg
Eisleben
Leipzig
Muhlberg
Ghent
Aachen
Marburg Castle
Wartburg Castle
Smalcald
Belgium
Mainz
Coburg
Czech Republic
Worms
Speyer
Heidelberg
Nuremberg
Luxembourg
Metz
Germany
Passau
Augsburg
Basel
Constance
Austria
Liechtenstein
France
Switzerland
Slovenia
La Bicocca
Pavia
Italy
Bologna
ADRIATIC SEA
Avignon
Florence
San Marino
PAPAL STATES
Monaco
Rome
Spain
MEDITERRANEAN SEA

1300

1305–1378
Papacy in Avignon, France.

Nov 10, 1483
Luther born in Eisleben.

1492
Columbus discovers America.

1502
Wittenberg University founded.

Nov 1, 1503
Julius II becomes pope.

Jul 2, 1505
Luther in thunderstorm vows to become monk.

Apr 18, 1506
Julius lays foundation for new St. Peter's.

Feb 21, 1513
Julius II dies.

1525

CHAPTER ONE

ROME, ITALY

APRIL 18, 1506

lmost nothing in history suddenly appears. The Reformation certainly did not. The causes of the Reformation stretch back centuries before Luther posted his protest on the church door in Wittenberg. The Roman papacy then was different from what it is today and different from what it was before the Great Schism in 1054—the event that separated the Eastern church from the Western church. The small apostolic church that spread through the Roman Empire grew to a large and powerful organization. Differences of opinion and teaching simmered even before the Great Schism. After the Schism, Constantinople was left as the center of the Eastern, or Orthodox, church and Rome, the Western, or Catholic, church.

According to Roman Catholic tradition, the bishop of Rome was a continuous succession of bishops who traced their origin to Peter's presence in Rome. Along with that assertion, Roman Catholics claim that the bishop of Rome always was the primary and universal head of western Christianity, even of all Christianity, including the Eastern church. Yes, a Christian bishop has existed in Rome or Avignon for centuries down to our own age. Yet differences of opinion continue to exist over the Roman pope's claim to primacy, in spite of Rome's persistent assertions.

The Rise of the Papacy

In the first centuries of the Christian church, the bishop of Rome was one of several important leaders in the church. When Constantine shifted the capitol of the Roman Empire to Constantinople, the affairs of the empire went with it. Rome remained important in the west as a cultural and religious center and even as a political center. Constantinople became important in the East as the new seat of the empire. It would also grow to be a cultural and religious center and rival of Rome. At the time that the empire moved eastward, Rome shared its importance as a Christian center with Jerusalem, Caesarea, Alexandria, and Antioch. Early councils of the church at Nicaea (325), Constantinople (381), Ephesus (431), and Chalcedon (451) convened in the east, and bishops from most Christian centers attended in order to decide important matters. Roman Catholic historians will naturally have a slightly different version of these events.

But dark clouds arose in the east. The storm of Islamic armies advanced from the desert to challenge Christian dominance. They conquered Alexandria (634), Jerusalem (637), Antioch (637), and Caesarea (638). The Christian light that came from these early Christian centers suddenly went dark. The Muslim advance continued across northern Africa and invaded Spain. Charles Martel stopped the Islamic armies at Tours in France (732). Islamic forces remained in Spain and also continued to challenge Christians in the east. They made their way toward Constantinople, but it stood against the Islamic armies for another 700 years.

These events had consequences. When Constantine moved his government to the East, a power vacuum plagued Europe. And then when the eastern Christian centers disappeared, Rome stood almost alone as a Christian center—alone certainly in Europe. It was quite natural for the bishop of Rome to assume leadership in the West. The rise of Christian Rome was a natural and necessary step. In many ways the presence of Roman spiritual and political power provided stability for the west. Sadly, over the next centuries, the Eastern and Western churches grew apart. In 1054 the patriarch of the Eastern church and the bishop of Rome excommunicated each other. Where there was once one Christian church with two great centers, there were now two separate churches—the Eastern Orthodox Church and the Roman Catholic Church. The Great Schism has remained a reality of history ever since.

At the time of the Schism, the bishop of Rome claimed universal supremacy over the entire church and asserted papal sovereignty and infallibility. But power corrupts, and the church is not immune to the principle. Good and dedicated leaders in the Western church occupied the papacy in earlier centuries, but eventually money, power, and pride corrupted the leadership of the church. The visible leader of the church ceased to be like Christ and his apostles. Instead the papacy became a wealthy political entity exercising great power. Even if one agrees with the claim that the pope can trace his origin to Peter, the pope was dramatically different from the simple fisherman of Galilee. The Vicar of Christ, living in luxury and extravagance, became more like Caesar than Christ. In fact, the papacy claimed that it was supreme even over kings and princes.

The Babylonian Captivity of the Papacy

As might be expected, because of the pope's temporal power and influence, the papacy was drawn into conflict with political leaders. Those leaders desired to control or to influence the papacy for their own agendas. In 1305 Clement V, a Frenchman, was elected pope. He chose not to move to Rome but to remain in France and moved his residence to Avignon. For about 70 years the papacy remained in Avignon. The popes during this time were all French and were influenced by the French crown. Rome was abandoned as the papal residence and lost its prestige. History calls this period the Babylonian Captivity of the Papacy because it lasted about 70 years, the same length of time the Babylonians held the Jews in captivity in the sixth century B.C.

Yet there is another dark chapter in the history of the papacy. After 70 years, tension between those who wished the papacy to remain in French territory and those who wanted it to return to Rome resulted in another schism. Beginning in 1378 and lasting for 40 more years, the church had two popes. One was in Avignon supported by the French and the other in Rome supported by the city-states of Italy, England, and others.

The scandal of two popes caused sincere and devout Christians to seek a solution. Many protested. Eventually these Christians concluded that only a council of the church could provide a solution. Three church councils were called to reform the church and heal the breach—the councils of Pisa, Constance, and Basel. Near the end of the schism, a third pope was the result of their efforts to solve the division. Eventually the councils succeeded. At the Council of Constance in 1417, Martin V was finally elected as pope to heal the schism. One of the rival popes resigned, and successors of the other faded away into history. The schism had been healed.

It was a sad chapter in the history of the Western church. Not only was there a struggle for dominance by rival popes, but other abuses also arose. The morals of the church officials and even many of the popes became notorious. The church that was centered in Avignon was extravagant, greedy, and corrupt. Financially, the Avignon papal court sought revenue in new ways that some considered excessive and oppressive. Selling church offices and indulgences were two of the strategies for raising the necessary funds to feed the appetites of Avignon. Sadly, these abuses did not disappear once the schism was healed. They continued even after the papacy was restored to Rome.

The second reform council, the Council of Constance (1414–1418), was the most important of the three councils for more reasons than the healing of the schism. Together with the councils of Pisa and Basel, it asserted power over the papacy. These councils claimed that the pope was subject to a council of the church and that the council of assembled Christians was superior to the pope and may even depose a pope for cause—revolutionary thoughts at the time. The question of whether popes could be wrong, and whether even councils could be wrong, became a part of the Reformation protest 100 years later when Luther posted his *95 Theses* and defended them against Roman papal claims.

The three reform councils were not only charged with healing the schism but also with instituting reforms to curb the other abuses of the hierarchy and papacy. The Council of Constance decided to postpone reform until the election of a new pope. Once that happened, the issue of reforms dropped down to unfinished business and received little official attention. It became old business at Basel with the same result. Finally, in spite of efforts to institute changes, the councils were not effective in curbing the financial or moral excesses of the papacy and the Roman curia.

Criticism and Protests

Already before the Babylonian Captivity of the Papacy, a resident of Florence raised his pen to write his protest in Italian, not Latin. Dante Alighieri (1265–1321) wrote *The Divine Comedy,* and within its Italian verses he included his own protest of the greed of the papacy. The *Comedy* tells the story of Dante's travels through hell, purgatory, and heaven. Dante is pictured as a visitor to hell and purgatory, guided by Virgil. Since Virgil was not a Christian, he could not serve as his guide in heaven. But as they traveled through hell, Dante and Virgil met former popes. These popes suffered hell for "buying and selling holy office." Hell also awaited the pope who was living in Dante's time. Dante's verses lament, "This avarice of yours grieves all the world, tramples the virtuous, and exalts the evil" (*Inferno* XIX, 98,99). Dante had been expelled from Florence and held a grudge against the pope, so one might excuse his comments as personal vendetta. Yet his condemnation of the papacy expressed the sentiments of his age.

Dante identified another of the problems that needed correction. In *Purgatory,* Dante depicts Marco, a Lombard who is paying for his faults. Marco comments on the papacy's political power. He says, "Tell the world this: The church of Rome, which fused two powers into one, has sunk in muck, defiling both herself and her true role" (XVI, 127-129). The two powers he identifies are the political power of the sword and the spiritual power of the cross.

In England, Chaucer (1340–1400) criticized the greed and hypocrisy of the clergy. The pardoner of the *Canterbury Tales* says boldly and without remorse, "My aim is all for gain and not at all for correction of sin." At the end of his tale, the pardoner pitches forgiveness, "My holy pardon will cure you all, provided that you offer nobles and others sterling coin, or else silver rings, brooches, spoons. . . . See, I enter your name here in my roll; you shall enter into heaven's bliss; I absolve you by my high power, you that will make offerings . . ." The pardoner's practice reminds anyone familiar with the Reformation of the sale of indulgences by John Tetzel in Germany.

Pope Julius II

After the Council of Constance resolved the schism by electing Pope Martin V, the issue of papal authority was not completely settled. Even the issue of who was the legitimate pope did not disappear. Reform was still on many agendas.

Martin V reluctantly called a council to address the needed reforms. The third council was to meet at Basel, but it did not convene until the year of Martin's death (1431). As feared by the pope, the Council of Basel asserted its authority over the papacy, requiring the pope to take an oath acknowledging the rights of the council, but Martin's successor, Eugene IV, tried to dissolve it and convene another rival council. That council excommunicated the prelates assembled at Basel. But the original Basel council responded by electing a rival pope, Felix V, who took the oath required by the council. He eventually resigned. The Council of Basel accomplished no significant reforms and adjourned in 1439. But Eugene sidestepped the issue of papal supremacy by his maneuvers and the failure of the Council of Basel.

From this point onward the popes continued to assert the superiority of the papacy over the councils. They chose to ignore the decrees of the reform councils, denounce them as heretical, or annul them. Several succeeding popes initiated reforms, but the needed reforms never came in sufficient strength. The abuses and corruption remained.

The history that played out over the next 100 years is an ongoing story of strong personalities, conflict, and intrigue filled with moral failings at the highest levels of the church, military alliances, and counter alliances. The rise of the Borgia family and Alexander VI (1492–1503) represent a stain on the papacy, a reality admitted by most even today. The struggle for dominance and the corruption left in its wake represent a disturbing chapter. Perhaps because of the corruption, many wanted reform even more desperately.

Julius II became pope after the shortest conclave in history—only a few hours—on October 31, 1503. In protest for the corrupt papacy of Alexander, he closed the quarters of Alexander VI and refused to enter them. Julius was an energetic, courageous leader whose focus was on reestablishing the political power of the papal states and on adding to the grandeur of Rome. He has been called the Warrior Pope, because he wore armor as he led papal armies against whatever enemy opposed his desire to consolidate the territory of the papal states. He is also called "terrible" because of his fierce determination, exacting nature, and violent temper.

When the papacy returned to Rome from Avignon, the city needed restoration. Buildings had deteriorated after the long history of neglect. So in spite of the corruption, the popes funded many improvements to Rome's churches, palaces, bridges, and other public buildings. The old St. Peter's Basilica built by Constantine was one of those churches in drastic need of repair. Rome had no church building to rival St. Mark's in Venice or St. Sophia in Constantinople. A few of the earlier popes had considered the renovation of Constantine's church in Rome. Pope Nicholas V (1447–1455) pulled down part of the ancient basilica and stored 2,522 cartloads of marble from the Coliseum for future construction.

However, it was up to Julius to take the dramatic step of removing the old St. Peter's Basilica completely and planning for a new one. On April 18, 1506, he laid the foundation stone for a new St. Peter's where the 1,000-year-old basilica of Constantine had once stood. What would rise from this event would be the largest and perhaps the most impressive church in the Christian world. That was the vision of Julius, but the rebuilding of St. Peter's would not be finished in his lifetime. It was finally consecrated on November 18, 1626, at enormous costs, spread out over those 120 years. In the process, Michelangelo, Raphael, and Bernini were among those who labored to make it what we see today. Both Raphael's work in the Vatican and Michelangelo's Sistine Chapel ceiling trace their origin back to Julius.

But another series of events would arise from the decision to rebuild St. Peter's—the Reformation. Julius wanted St. Peter's to be the centerpiece of a new Rome. Of course, the massive building project required money. Julius asked for large contributions from European kings and instituted the sale of indulgences to pay for the building project. The decision to issue these indulgences was not difficult, nor was it an unusual strategy for raising money; indulgences had a long history for the papacy. They had been used already during the Crusades to encourage soldiers to fight against the Muslims and to raise money for their campaigns. St Peter's rose with the help of the money raised from the indulgences Julius authorized. Leo X, the successor of Julius, renewed the indulgences, and the appeal for funds spread to Germany, creating the spark for Luther's protest.

One more interesting series of events bring together Julius II, indulgences, and Frederick the Wise of Saxony. Elector Ernst of Saxony, Frederick's father, died as a result of a hunting accident in 1486, making Frederick the new elector. In these early days Frederick became deeply involved in imperial politics and for a time served as an imperial governor under Emperor Maximilian. But he left Maximilian and turned his attention to his home in Saxony. He founded the University of Wittenberg in 1502 and included the Castle Church (All Saints) in his building plans in Saxony. Frederick spent more than a little effort on the collection of an impressive array of relics. In 1507 Julius II appealed to the imperial estates to bequeath their relics to Frederick. Some of the relics were always on display. All of Frederick's 5,005 relics were on display on the Monday after Misericordias Domini Sunday—two weeks after Easter. Those who came received indulgences for their pilgrimage. On April 8, 1510, Julius issued two papal bulls for All Saints Church that would even increase the indulgences pilgrims could acquire by coming to Wittenberg to view the relics (Wellman 130-1). ❦

NORTH SEA

BALTIC SEA

1000

1184
Peter Waldo excommunicated.

Dec 31, 1384
John Wycliffe dies.

Lutterworth

Jul 6, 1415
Jan Hus burned at the stake, executed for heresy by the Council of Constance.

Wittenberg

London

ENGLISH CHANNEL

May 23, 1498
Savonarola executed in Florence.

Basel

Constance

1512
Michelangelo finishes Sistine Chapel ceiling.

Mar 1, 1516
Erasmus publishes Greek New Testament. Humanist scholar, supported Reformation at first.

ADRIATIC SEA

Florence

1524
Erasmus publishes *On Free Will.*

Rome

1525

MEDITERRANEAN SEA

CHAPTER TWO

BASEL, SWITZERLAND

MARCH 1, 1516

he Luther Monument in Worms, Germany, is the largest Luther monument in the world. Thanks to contributions from Lutherans all around the world, it was dedicated on June 22, 1868. Ernest Rietschel's design places Luther in the center surrounded by a low wall. On each corner of the wall stand figures of key Reformation characters. On one corner stands Frederick the Wise of Saxony and on another Philip of Hesse, two powerful princes who played a major role in the Reformation. Behind Luther on the other two corners stand Johann Reuchlin and Philip Melanchthon, two important Reformation scholars.

At Luther's feet, four men face outward—Peter Waldo, John Wycliffe, Jan Hus, and Girolamo Savonarola. Before Luther's protest at Wittenberg, they issued their own protests against the teaching and practice of the Roman Church. All four of them in one way or another wanted the church to abandon the practices that had evolved over the centuries.

Peter Waldo

Peter Waldo (1140–1218) appeared long before the Reformation—over one hundred years before the Babylonian Captivity of the Papacy (1305–1378). He reminded Christians of the value and importance of simplicity and poverty. In the excesses of the Roman Church of his day, he saw a church that had moved away from the simplicity and teaching of Jesus. The simplicity of the Galilean fisherman, Peter, also stood in stark contrast to the pomp and luxury of the church of Waldo's day. His message was a protest against the excesses of the popes and Roman Catholic officials.

Waldo and his followers adhered strictly to the Bible. He has been credited with the first translation of the Bible into a spoken language (Arpitan) instead of Latin. He opposed the Roman doctrines of purgatory and transubstantiation. His followers were referred to as the Poor of Lyons, because they spread their teaching while dressed as peddlers. In response, the Roman Church persecuted him and his followers. Many were sentenced to death.

John Wycliffe

John Wycliffe (1320–1384), however, lived during those difficult days when the papacy moved from Rome to Avignon. He is sometimes called the "morning star of the Reformation." Born in Yorkshire, England, Wycliffe was trained at Oxford, which became the principal seat of his work. During his time the Black Plague ravaged England and Europe, leaving about one-third of the population dead.

In England, the papacy owned a third of the land and was exempt from taxes. It was said that the pope received five times as much money as the king. Because the pope was in Avignon and under the influence, if not the control of, the French king, the protest was natural for the English.

Wycliffe served on a committee that went to the Netherlands to discuss the issues created by the flow of money from England to the papacy. That experience led him to conclude that the papal representatives were greedy, corrupt, and certainly a tool of the French crown. Wycliffe suggested that the true pope was one whose teaching and life most nearly followed Jesus and Saint Peter. Like other protesters, he thought that the church should give up its worldly possessions and return to the patterns of the early church. Neither Peter nor Christ had grandeur, might, or political power. He had no difficulty siding with the English king in withholding money from Rome. He went on also to condemn purgatory and the selling of indulgences.

Wycliffe professed another view that put him at odds with the pope. He taught that Christ and the Bible were the only authority for the Christian. Wycliffe was among the first in many centuries to teach the absolute authority of the Scriptures against the Roman assertion that the pope was the ultimate authority. Because he believed in the authority of the Scriptures, he thought it was important for the common man to read them. So he translated the Bible into English, basing his translation on the Latin translation of Jerome, the Vulgate. He is perhaps best known for his work on the English translation of the Bible. Placing Scripture in the hands of the common laity was forbidden by the church of his day. To the church leaders at the time, placing the Bible into the language of common people desecrated what was holy. The Bible was considered a book for the clergy, who were to interpret its meaning for the people.

Similar to Waldo and his followers, the Roman Church opposed Wycliffe and his followers. Yet the ideas of Wycliffe found many willing adherents in England. His followers were called the Lollards, who went out two by two wearing long dark red robes and carrying staffs. Their influence grew in spite of the efforts of the Roman Church to suppress them. Exasperated by their spread, one church leader suggested that every second man he met was a Lollard. Wycliffe did not suffer a martyr's end. He suffered a stroke from which he did not recover and died in December 1384. Yet the Roman Catholic Church did not forget his protest. He would be on the agenda of the Council of Constance (1414–1418).

Jan Hus

Like-minded Christians did not forget Wycliffe either. His influence spread to Bohemia through the Bohemian students who attended Oxford, the center of Wycliffe's efforts. Jan Hus (1369–1415) was one of those students. He is the third protestor below Luther on the memorial in Worms. His position with Luther came through the influence of Wycliffe's ideas. Jan Hus translated some of Wycliffe's work into Czech and circulated them in Bohemia because he was a champion of the use of the language of the people. His translation of Wycliffe's works found an eager audience in Prague.

Hus protested the morals of the clergy and the papacy and became the chief defender of Wycliffe's ideas in Prague. Like others before them, Wycliffe and Hus proposed a different view of the church. The church was not the Roman pope and the clergy hierarchy, but instead it was the gathering of the elect—the believers. Their claim was that the church had existed without the pope and cardinals for hundreds of years. These ideas were not new or unheard of before Hus or Wycliffe. Over the centuries, others had expressed them. Hus also challenged the assertion that the church was built on Peter. He sided with Augustine in maintaining that Peter was never the foundation rock of the holy Catholic Church but, rather, that the church was built on Christ.

When the pope sought to finance a war against his enemies through the sale of indulgences (1411), Hus challenged the sale of indulgences. He suggested that the pope should not wage war at all but should pray for his enemies and adhere to the words of Jesus: "My kingdom is not of this world" (John 18:36).

The ideas of Jan Hus set him on a collision course with the Roman Church. His protest against the abuses brought condemnation. His books were burned. But the ideas of Hus gained adherents and persisted in spite of the opposition of the Roman Church. Husites remained to Luther's day, 100 years later. Jan Hus, on the other hand, died a martyr at the Council of Constance (1415). Sigismund, the emperor at the time, had promised him safe-conduct to appear before the council. But he was imprisoned and treated with disdain and contempt. Yet he did not recant. For his refusal to recant, he was sentenced to death. At the place of his execution, straw and wood were heaped up to his chin. Just before the torch was set to the wood and straw, the executioner offered him one last chance to recant. He replied, "I shall die with joy today in the faith of the gospel I have preached." Fire consumed his life, body, clothes, and shoes. His ashes were thrown into the Rhine so that there would be no relics.

Wycliffe had died 20 years earlier, but the Council of Constance also considered his connection with Hus. The council ordered that John Wycliffe's bones be exhumed, burned, and the ashes thrown into the River Swift in England. As far as the established church was concerned, it believed that it had pleased God by destroying the Bohemian heretic and his English teacher. For them the protest was over, and business went on as usual.

Girolamo Savonarola

Protests, however, were not over. Florence was the home of the Dominican friar, Savonarola (1452–1498). His position at the Luther Monument might be surprising to some. He was a true Roman Catholic in many ways. When he died he considered himself Roman Catholic, but he died a martyr for his beliefs. He was a remarkable figure and protested the sins of the pope and the Roman curia. His sermons attracted large crowds in Florence as he issued dramatic and powerful calls to repent. Support for his message came from his character, which was beyond reproach, and from his preaching.

When he attacked the morals of the clergy and the Vatican, he stirred the hornet's nest. From Florence, he pointed to Rome where he charged that offices were sold to the highest bidder and where the palaces of the clergy were full of tapestries, silk, and perfumes. He accused the clergy of polluting the sacraments by requiring payments. He was deeply familiar with the Scriptures, and his sermons were filled with the prophetic message of future judgment, echoing the theme of many of the Old Testament prophets.

But the pope was determined to silence him. Savonarola refused to come to Rome when beckoned by the pope (Alexander VI). Eventually, the pope, without evidence, accused him of heresy. The truth was that he was not a heretic. He professed belief in the seven Roman Catholic sacraments, but he had rebelled against the Roman hierarchy and the pope when he refused to obey the directives of the pope.

He was eventually silenced. Proclaimed a heretic, imprisoned, and tortured, he and two others were hanged in Florence. Their bodies were burned and their ashes cast into the Arno River. At his execution, when told that he would be separated from the church militant and the church triumphant, he defiantly said that he would indeed not be separated from the church triumphant because the Roman priest did not have the power to separate him from heaven.

Two reasons are often given for his inclusion among the others in the Luther Monument at Worms. First, he understood the grace of God in Christ. He believed that God's grace was not obtained by works of merit. Instead, salvation came solely by the goodness of God. He wrote, "Tell me, Peter; tell me, O Magdalene, why are you in paradise? Confess that not by your own merits have you obtained salvation, but by the goodness of God" (Schaff 6, 715).

Second, Luther published Savonarola's *Meditations* on Psalm 51 and 32, which the Florentine preacher wrote just before his execution. Luther declared them "a piece of evangelical teaching and Christian piety. For, in them Savonarola is seen entering in not as a Dominican monk, trusting in his vows, the rules of his order, his cowl and masses and good works but clad in the breastplate of righteousness and armed with the shield of faith and the helmet of salvation, not as a member of the Order of Preachers but as an everyday Christian" (Schaff 6, 711). Grace was central. The last words of the two men executed with Savonarola were "Jesus, Jesus." Salvation by grace was and is not an exclusive Lutheran idea. It is a Christian idea that stretches back to the ancient church and crosses denominational boundaries.

Savonarola's protest illustrates one more reality about the Roman Catholic Church at the time of the Reformation. Protests came from many different quarters. The church was arrogant, greedy, and corrupt; almost everyone knew it. The Babylonian Captivity of the Papacy and the Great Schism were symptoms. Savonarola, a defender of the Catholic faith, was brutal in his criticism. He was silenced by the hangman's rope in Florence. Yet centuries later there were supporters of him in the Roman Church who urged his canonization.

The church, at the time of Savonarola and later, was in desperate need of reform. The councils called to carry out the reform were one attempt for

Christians to change and reform the papacy and the hierarchy. Yet while reform was on the agenda of all three reform councils, reform never reached the top of the agenda. It was difficult to tackle the thorny problem of real reform. Sadly, the needed reforms never came. If they had, the Reformation may never have taken place.

In addition to these men, other voices had criticized the church. The Franciscans were faithful Roman Catholic monks quietly working in the Western church. They were dedicated to poverty and chastity. Although still ensnared by distortions of the biblical truth, their pure and simple life was a stark contrast to the luxury, grandeur, and affluence of the Roman curia and the pope—a quiet protest that was in sharp contrast to existing conditions.

Erasmus and the Greek New Testament

Much closer to the Reformation, Erasmus joined the protest against the clergy. Erasmus was the son of a priest, Gerard, born most likely in 1466. His mother may have been the priest's housekeeper, Margarethe Rogerius (perhaps Rutgers). Little may be known for sure, but he was cared for by both his parents until their early death from the plague in 1483. He received the best education possible at that time in schools run by the monks. He became not only a priest but also an eminent scholar and a champion of humanism. He spoke and wrote to free scholarship from its medieval formalism and purify it by returning it to the original sources. Part of that emphasis led him to learn Greek and emphasize the importance of the original languages of the Scriptures.

While he and Luther both had a desire to see the church reformed, Erasmus remained loyal to the Roman Catholic Church. In his *Praise of Folly,* Erasmus did not hesitate to mock scholastic theologians. He wrote that they "haven't even a spare moment in which to read even once through the gospel or the letters of Paul" (Section 53, 161). He described the supreme pontiffs as those "who are so occupied with their monetary harvests [they] delegate all their more apostolic work to the bishops, the bishops to the heads of the churches and these to their vicars; they in turn . . . in the hands of those who will shear the sheep's wool" (Section 119, 183). Erasmus, like Dante, Chaucer, and many others, protested the abuses but also understood that there was good in the church. Erasmus said he did not intend to "censure the good" (Section 119, 183).

His interest in the original languages of Scripture led him to the Greek manuscripts of the New Testament. While Luther lectured in Wittenberg, Erasmus provided the church with an edition of the Greek New Testament.

Before Erasmus, the accepted translation of the original languages of Scripture was the Latin Vulgate. Most likely sometime in 1514 or 1515 he decided to work on a Greek New Testament and came to Basel to accomplish it. He used most of the manuscripts available to him in Basel to produce his edition. It went to the printer on October 2, 1515, and was finished on March 1, 1516. The book was bilingual, with Greek in the left column and Latin in the right. His goal was to validate the Vulgate by including the Greek. The first edition was hurried into print, so it was filled with errors. Another edition followed in 1519 that corrected most of the errors. The final and fifth edition was printed in 1535, a year before his death. Luther no doubt used the Greek text of Erasmus to translate the New Testament when he was confined to the Wartburg from May 1521 to March 1522.

Erasmus represented an emerging emphasis in the church at the time. Not all who objected to the practices of the church would agree with Luther. Yet they shared his desire to change what had evolved since the time of the apostles and especially what had grown up in the place of the apostolic church. Interest in the ancient languages was an important contribution.

By the time Erasmus published his New Testament in Greek, Luther had become a monk and a priest. He had traveled to Rome on behalf of the Augustinians in 1510. He had earned his degree as doctor of theology and been assigned to the University of Wittenberg to teach the Bible (1512). He had yet to be noticed. But reform was in the air, and many waited for the coming of someone who would be the catalyst. The church leaders before Luther resisted change and silenced the voices that sought to improve the church. The story is told that when Jan Hus died, he told the executioner that he could kill this goose (*Hus* in Bohemian means "goose") but in 100 years a swan will come after him that no one will be able to silence. His words seemed to prophesy that after his death another would come to fulfill the dream of reformation. It was a hope many retained in the face of the grim reality of persecution. Yet while many longed for reformation of God's church on earth, God would ultimately decide whether the protests would succeed or continue to be snuffed out. ❦

1500

1510
Luther sent to Rome.

Oct 1512
Luther earns doctor of theology.

Mar 9, 1513
Leo X becomes pope.

1514
Albert borrows money for church offices and authorized to sell indulgences.

Jan 22, 1517
Turks take Cairo, Egypt.

Oct 31, 1517
Luther posts 95 Theses.

Aug 25, 1518
Melanchthon arrives in Wittenberg to teach Greek.

1525

CHAPTER THREE

WITTENBERG, GERMANY

OCTOBER 31, 1517

One monk with a rolled-up document in one hand and a hammer in the other calmly walked down the main street in Wittenberg. No one bothered to notice as he walked through the town square on his way to the Castle Church. They had other more important things to do in the market. Besides, they knew this monk; he was a teacher in the new university there and was simply going to post some notice for the university. The monk was Martin Luther.

They were right. Martin Luther unrolled the announcement and nailed it to the door of the church. He posted a series of theses for debate and scholarly discussion at the university. The theses were in Latin, so town people couldn't even read them. The theses protested the abuses connected with the sale of indulgences in Germany. The indulgences in question were not even for sale in Saxony where Luther lived and worked, but people were crossing the border into neighboring territory in order to buy them. They returned to Wittenberg with strange ideas about guilt, forgiveness, and the value of indulgences. Luther was asked for his opinion on these matters. So he studied to find answers and came to different conclusions than those of the indulgence sellers. He became convinced that the sale of indulgences in Germany had been abused and sought to correct the abuse. The result was the *95 Theses* posted on the door of the church.

Indulgences Come to Germany

Indulgences were not new in the church. They had been used already during the Crusades to encourage soldiers to fight against the Muslims and to raise money for their campaigns. The practice grew from the Roman sacrament of Penance. When sinners confessed their sins to a priest, he forgave the guilt of the sin before God. But that was not the end of it. The priest then also imposed some satisfaction to be performed to validate the sincerity of the penitent so the forgiveness offered would actually apply to the sinner. Indulgences, in the strict sense of the term, were the removal of the requirement of these earthly satisfactions. They were not intended to forgive the guilt of sin but to remove the church's required satisfaction imposed on sinners not only in this life but also in purgatory.

The popes had used indulgences before. Julius II followed the existing practice and authorized indulgences for the building of Saint Peter's. The basilica would grow into one of the largest and most beautiful churches in the Christian world, and of course, it would be expensive. So Julius II authorized the sale of indulgences. When Leo X became pope, he inherited a full papal treasury from Julius. But Leo spent the money on art, feasts, and entertaining. In addition, he conducted a war to advance the political fortunes of his family, the Medici, and the papal states. The war ended in September 1517 and wrecked papal finances. It is said that Leo spent the financial resources of three popes—Julius II, his own, and his successor. For Leo X, finances remained a nagging problem. He sold church offices and borrowed large sums from bankers and others just as earlier popes did. Like some of the others, his need for funds also led to the sale of indulgences.

One of those who paid for a new church office had a direct bearing on the Reformation and Luther's protest. He was Albert. In 1513 he had become both Archbishop of Magdeburg and the Bishop of Halberstadt at the age of 23. It was illegal to hold more than one church office, but Pope Leo X received financial consideration from Albert and then granted him a dispensation to become both Archbishop of Magdeburg and Bishop of Halberstadt. But the scenario was not yet finished. Albert and his family wanted the power and prestige of the leading church position in Germany. They sought to make Albert also the Archbishop of Mainz when it became available.

After a series of negotiations, Leo and Albert agreed on a fee for the third office. In order to pay the fees, Albert borrowed money from the Fruggers, a wealthy merchant and banking family in Germany. This paved the way for Pope Leo X to announce a sale of indulgences not only to finance Albert's new position but also to continue the building of Saint Peter's in Rome. Albert commissioned John Tetzel, among others, to conduct the sale. Tetzel, the most famous, was good at his job. The bankers paid him well and even accompanied Tetzel and the others to check expenses and make sure they received their share.

As part of his office, Archbishop Albert wrote instructions for the salesmen and stressed among other things that these indulgences were full indulgences for the living and the dead. Tetzel marched into the towns of Germany with banners, candles, and singing. He often preached a sermon on hell in the town square and then went to the church where he preached another sermon on purgatory. His third sermon was on heaven. His tactics and message created eager purchasers who desired to escape hell and purgatory themselves or help their departed family members to enter heaven.

The three topics for these sermons followed the medieval religious concepts that had developed in the church. The three parts of Dante's *Divine Comedy* are arranged on the concepts of the church of his day—Inferno (hell), Purgatory, and Paradise—and it also assumes the progression of a soul from purgatory to heaven. The number of years spent in purgatory to pay the satisfaction for sin was enormous. As those thousands and millions of years passed, each soul in purgatory slowly progressed toward paradise. Indulgences shortened those years. Of course, the souls in heaven achieved their state by their special devotion to God in this life or by completing their time in purgatory. Neither purgatory nor the practice of indulgences is based on any New Testament or Old Testament Scripture. Instead, both are based on tradition and the authority of the Roman Church and its pope.

Luther's Protest

Stories of Tetzel's exaggerations and abuses while selling indulgences are easy to find. Tetzel's little jingle was on the lips of many: "As soon as the money clinks in the chest, the soul flits into heavenly rest." Some of those who returned from purchasing indulgences believed that the indulgences were tickets to heaven, and others believed that if they purchased an indulgence they no longer needed to practice Christian virtues. These distortions persisted because the sale of indulgences was protected from opposition by the authority of the church. Anyone who opposed Tetzel was threatened with excommunication—a power given to him to assure his success and inspire fear in anyone who would frustrate his efforts.

Nevertheless, Luther objected. He was interested not in overthrowing the church of his day but in challenging and correcting the abuses so evident in the practice of selling indulgences. His goal was to protect the Christian believers he served in Wittenberg. The document posted on the door of the church in Wittenberg was written in Latin, the language of scholars, and intended for discussion with scholars. At this point Luther desired to start a dialog that would curb the abuses. Luther sent a copy of his *Theses* to Archbishop Albert with a letter asking him to stop the sale of indulgences.

The *Theses* did not remain in the dusty domain of scholars. No one stepped forward to debate Luther's thesis. Instead they were quickly translated into German and within two weeks seemed to have circulated into every corner of Germany. Within four weeks they had found an audience far beyond Germany. It seems that many objected not only to the abuses of the sale of indulgences but also to the reach of the Roman curia into the pockets of people all over Europe.

But Luther's protest was more than just a protest against Rome's avarice. Underneath it was a deeper question about the validity of indulgences and the authority behind them. This serious challenge to Rome's authority and structure became more than the simple echo of a hammer on the door of the Castle Church. It was to shake the very foundations of the church of 1517. Luther wrote,

- The pope cannot remit any guilt, except by declaring and showing that it has been remitted by God. (Thesis 6)
- They preach only human doctrines who say that as soon as the money clinks into the money chest, the soul flies out of purgatory. (Thesis 27)
- Men must especially be on their guard against those who say that the pope's pardons are that inestimable gift of God by which man is reconciled to him. (Thesis 33)
- Any truly repentant Christian has a right to full remission of penalty and guilt even without indulgence letters. (Thesis 36)
- [The indulgences] are nevertheless in truth the most insignificant graces when compared with the grace of God and the piety of the cross. (Thesis 68)
- To say that the cross emblazoned with the papal coat of arms and set up by the indulgence preachers is equal in worth to the cross of Christ is blasphemy. (Thesis 79)
- To repress these very sharp arguments of the laity by force alone, and not to resolve them by giving reasons, is to expose the church and the pope to the ridicule of their enemies and make Christians unhappy. (Thesis 90)

Luther had not come to these conclusions suddenly. Yes, a bolt of lightning did suddenly change his course years before. While studying to be a lawyer and traveling from home back to Erfurt, he was caught in a severe thunderstorm. In 1505 a sudden bolt of lightning caused Luther to erupt in fear with a vow to become a monk. Shortly after, back safely at Erfurt, he abandoned the wishes of his father to pursue law, sold his belongings, and entered the Augustinian monastery. Luther progressed in his studies and gained a good reputation. During the papacy of Julius II, he was even sent to Rome seeking a papal solution to a dispute among the Augustinian monasteries in Germany.

Later, he was sent to Wittenberg where he earned his doctorate and lectured. His workload increased rapidly. On October 26, 1516, he wrote to his friend John Lang, "I nearly need two copyists or secretaries. All day long I do almost nothing else than write letters; therefore I am sometimes not aware of whether or not I constantly repeat myself, but you will see. I am a preacher at the monastery, I am a reader during mealtimes, I am asked daily to preach in the city church, I have to supervise the study [of novices and friars], I am a vicar (and that means I am eleven times prior), I am caretaker of the fish [pond] at Leitskau, I represent the people of Herzberg at the court in Torgau, I lecture on Paul, and I am assembling [material for] a commentary on the Psalms" (AE 48, 27-8).

At this time, Luther was also growing in his theological insight. He began to develop an understanding of the Scriptures as the sole authority in theology. While Luther was teaching at Wittenberg, his focus began to center on the importance of Christ. What has been called his tower discovery was the dawn of his understanding of justification. At the beginning of his studies, Luther had considered the "righteousness of God" a fierce standard by which God evaluates human effort and punishes the sinner. Since his thunderbolt experience, Luther had been trying to gain the righteousness he understood God demanded from him. According to the church's view, God could not declare anyone righteous who was not righteous. So according to the Roman Church's teaching, to have the required righteousness, one must earn it by works pleasing to God or receive it from the treasury of the saints—that is, the surplus of good deeds done by the saints. Baptism started the process of gaining enough righteousness, and the Mass contributed to the process as well. Luther believed that his decision to be a monk, his prayers, and rigorous discipline all were gaining righteousness. But it would not be enough. The church taught that even after death his soul would need the prayers of others and Masses performed for his progress through purgatory.

As he was preparing lectures on Paul's letter to the Romans, Luther was struck by Paul's words: "For in the gospel a righteousness from God is revealed, a righteousness that is by faith from first to last, just as it is written: 'The righteous will live by faith'" (Romans 1:17). These words seemed so different from what he had previously understood by the righteousness of God. As he mulled over the words, a new insight overtook him: righteousness was not earned but was instead a gift from God for Christ's sake, which comes from God to the sinner by faith. In other words, God justifies the sinner—proclaims the sinner righteous by faith. Luther felt that once he understood this concept, he had "entered Paradise through widely open doors."

Armed with this new insight, his lectures more and more abandoned the teachings of the traditional scholastic theologians. He found reassurance of his insight in the writings of St. Augustine, a fourth-century bishop of Hippo in northern Africa, who was one of the key church fathers of the Roman Church. Luther looked for what would advance the cause of Christ and the grace of God. The insight caused a shift in his thinking that was noticeable at the University of Wittenberg. He commented to his friend in a letter dated May 18, 1517:

> Our theology and St. Augustine are progressing well, and with God's help rule at our University. Aristotle is gradually falling from his throne, and his final doom is only a matter of time. It is amazing how the lectures on the *Sentences* [the standard textbook for theology in the Middle Ages] are disdained. Indeed no one can expect to have any students if he does not want to teach this theology, that is, lecture on the Bible or on St. Augustine or another teacher of ecclesiastical eminence. (AE 48, 42)

The *95 Theses* grew from his deepening understanding of the righteousness of God. Because the *95 Theses* were in Latin and a part of the academic practice of university life, it should not surprise us that they were not noticed right away by most of the people in Wittenberg. But once they had been translated and spread beyond the university, they took on a life of their own. Luther's words became the spark that ignited the hoped-for flame of reformation. Different reactions were quick to come. Elector Frederick the Wise, Luther's sovereign, supported his doctor of theology and university teacher. Emperor Maximilian, the grandfather of Charles V who would become emperor shortly, at first felt that Luther might be a powerful ally for Germany against Rome. He later changed his mind about Luther. When the *Theses* arrived in Rome, they were dismissed as nothing more than a monkish squabble. Leo himself was amused and predicted that the German monk would sing a different tune soon. He also changed his mind and soon took steps to silence Luther.

1500

Apr 26, 1518
Luther participates in Heidelberg Disputation.

Oct 12-14, 1518
Luther meets with Cajetan in Augsburg.

Nov 9, 1518
Leo X clarifies indulgence practice.

Dec 8, 1518
Frederick refuses to turn over Luther without a hearing on German soil.

Sep 20, 1519
Magellan begins voyage around the world.

1525

North Sea
Baltic Sea
Wittenberg
London
Wartburg Castle
English Channel
Heidelberg
Augsburg
Adriatic Sea
Rome
Mediterranean Sea

CHAPTER FOUR

AUGSBURG, GERMANY

OCTOBER 12-14, 1518

ope Leo X at first felt the *95 Theses* represented a monk's squabble far away in Germany—an argument between the Dominicans who conducted the sale of indulgences and the Augustinians. Tetzel, a Dominican, of course was among the first to defend the sale of indulgences. Early in 1518, the Dominicans met at Frankfurt. Tetzel was made Doctor of Theology and presented a series of theses in support of indulgences. His theses offered no support for indulgences from Scripture but instead built a case for them on papal authority and obedience to the pope. The Dominicans claimed that in a short time Luther would be burned at the stake.

Leo soon altered his approach from amusement to opposition. He took steps to silence Luther. The problem was that he not only underestimated Luther but also did not grasp the full significance of the protest. In Wittenberg, Luther went about his daily tasks while the *Theses* were published and republished throughout Europe. They became the topic of discussion far beyond Wittenberg and Saxony. Luther's protest found eager readers who supported his thoughts. What happened was not just a squabble between Dominicans and Augustinians. Nevertheless, Leo gave instructions for the Augustinians to silence their German monk. Rome gave the task to John Staupitz, the leader of the Saxon Augustinians who earlier had encouraged Luther to cling to Christ in the midst of his anguish over sin.

Heidelberg and Prierias' *Dialogue*

But Leo's first efforts were not enough. More needed to be done to silence Luther and quash his ideas and prevent them from spreading. In spring of 1518 Luther and Leonhard Beier traveled from Wittenberg to Heidelberg for the triennial gathering of the Augustinians. Already Luther's friends were concerned about him and his safety, but Luther and Beier walked to Heidelberg under the protection of Elector Frederick. Once in Heidelberg, Staupitz began the meeting on April 25 but avoided a direct discussion of the controversial topic of indulgences. Instead, Luther and Beier were asked to debate other theses on original sin, grace, free will, and faith.

In the discussion, Luther clarified the difference between the theology of glory and the theology of the cross and began to express what his tower discovery had taught him. He wrote, "He is not righteous who does much, but he who, without work, believes much in Christ" (Heidelberg Thesis 25 AE 31, 55) and "The law says, 'do this,' and it is never done. Grace says, 'believe in this,' and everything is already done" (Heidelberg Thesis 26 AE 31, 56). Luther had abandoned the Roman Church's dependence on works and its thinking about satisfaction. He had centered his thinking on the work of Christ: "The person who believes that he can obtain grace by doing what is in him adds sin to sin so that he becomes doubly guilty" (Heidelberg Thesis 16 AE 31, 50). The protest against indulgences expanded to those teachings that had moved the church away from the Scriptures and the church of the apostles.

Many of the older Augustinians resisted the approach of Luther, but the younger men supported Luther and were impressed with his character, scholarship, and grasp of both church history and Scripture. He did not need to walk back to Wittenberg but returned in a wagon provided by friends.

Yet Luther still believed that his protest did not go beyond what the Roman Catholic Church always believed. He felt that Leo X was unaware of the indulgence abuses and distortions in Germany. Luther believed that the indulgence traffic was a problem with the Dominicans and Tetzel rather than the papacy. He remained humble and submissive to Leo X. He promised Staupitz that he would complete an explanation of the *95 Theses* and send it to Rome. In that explanation he wrote, "I testify that I desire to say or maintain absolutely nothing except, first of all, what is in the Holy Scriptures and can be maintained from them; and then what is in the form and writings of the church fathers and is accepted by the Roman Church preserved both in the cannons and the papal decrees" (AE 31, 83).

But when Leo received Luther's explanation, he was already initiating formal proceedings against Luther. He appointed Sylvester Prierias to respond to Luther's *Theses.* Prierias was a Dominican theological expert and an official advisor to Leo X. He boasted that it took him only three days to draft his response, *Dialogue*. But while it came from official circles in the Vatican, it didn't say much more than Tetzel said earlier. Prierias maintained that the Church of Rome could make decisions and anyone who thinks differently than Rome was a heretic. He also suggested that anyone who did not accept the Church of Rome and the pope as an infallible rule of faith was guilty of heresy.

Debate or discussion of the issues was out of the question. Instead it became a case of bullying Luther: agree with us or we will destroy you by calling you a heretic and excommunicating you. Later, Rome would give Luther only one choice, retract your protest or become an outlaw subject to excommunication and death. Rome was repeating the approach it took with Jan Hus at the Council of Constance a hundred years earlier. Luther considered Prierias' critique of little significance and suggested that only the Holy Scriptures were without error. At one point he suggested that Prierias should not attempt to write any more books lest he embarrass himself.

Another document reached Luther with Prierias' *Dialogue*—a summons to Rome. Luther received the documents on August 7 and was directed to appear in Rome within 60 days for interrogation. Everyone knew what the Roman curia saw as the end of the Luther problem. A high Vatican official had already declared him a heretic. All that remained was for Luther simply to face interrogation and execution in Rome and his protest would disappear. The world of politics would now play a role in preventing the Roman Church from its plan to arrest Luther, bind him hand and foot, and bring him to Rome.

Two Worlds Collide: Augsburg 1518

Frederick, the elector of Saxony, stood in the way of Rome's plan. He exerted his influence with the emperor to have Luther heard on German soil. So Leo X chose another attempt to silence the German monk. He turned to the most respected theologian in the church of his day. Tommaso de Vio (Cajetan), a Dominican cardinal, who was already in Augsburg and also received the *Dialogue* of Prierias and the summons directing Luther to appear in Rome. Cajetan was at the Imperial Diet of Emperor Maximilian I on a special assignment of the pope to gain acceptance for an imperial tax to fund a crusade against the Turks. Egypt had fallen into the hands of the Turks in 1517. That Turkish victory created a powerful adversary in the East and exposed Hungary, Austria, Italy, and much of the Mediterranean world to attack by the Muslims. Cardinal Cajetan was also in Augsburg to stoke the fire of opposition to Luther and turn Maximilian and the others against the German heretic.

What made matters especially difficult for Luther was a forged set of theses on the papal ban supposedly written by Luther. A companion forgery attributed to Luther that bitterly attacked the Roman curia also appeared. Maximilian saw the forgeries, deemed them genuine, and wrote a letter to Leo X urging immediate action against Luther. Leo sent directions to Cajetan to arrest Luther, absolve him if he recanted, and, if not, place him under the ban, which meant excommunication, and the interdict, which meant that all Luther's supporters would also be subject to excommunication if they continued to support him. Leo X sent a letter to Frederick the Wise asking for his help to arrest Luther, the "son of perdition" as his letter described him.

Cajetan's reputation was rock solid. In 1511 two rival councils struggled over whether a church council or the papacy was the supreme authority. The Council of Pisa, called a pseudo council by Roman Catholic historians, maintained that church councils were supreme. The Fifth Lateran Council maintained that the pope was supreme. In the controversy, Cajetan defended the power and supremacy of the papacy. He was a master of sacred theology and taught the theology of Thomas Aquinas. Beginning in 1507 and finishing in 1522, he wrote commentaries on Thomas Aquinas. He was a refined gentleman with the presence of importance and leadership.

When Luther received the summons to Rome, he appealed to Elector Frederick the Wise hoping for a change of venue—a neutral German court where the issues could be discussed fairly. Frederick understood that the documents that caused such a reaction from Maximilian were forgeries, and he became a key player in this drama at this point. He was one of the seven electors who would cast a vote for the next emperor. At this time, Maximilian, at age 59, was promoting his grandson Charles as the next emperor and needed Frederick's support. Leo X and the Roman curia were not ready to agree with Maximilian and give such power to Charles. They feared that they might lose their own power in Italy. So they supported Francis I in his candidacy as emperor. This tension pitted emperor against the pope and Francis. Eventually Charles would be elected, but not without a political struggle. When Charles was elected to succeed his grandfather, the conflict would continue for many years and create a German bubble where the Reformation would flourish.

For now, however, another collision grew on the horizon. Frederick was a veteran of imperial politics already. He had served at Maximilian's court and had been Elector Frederick of Saxony since 1486. With the help of jurists, Luther had asked for a hearing in the empire, a legal appeal that prevented his immediate transfer to Rome. Maximilian, who at first sided with the pope against Luther, now, in response to the pope's refusal to endorse the plan for his grandson, opposed the pope. When Frederick proposed that Luther be heard on German soil, a compromise was reached. Cajetan suggested that he would conduct the interview with Luther himself in Augsburg. He promised that he would exercise a fatherly attitude toward the German monk, but he still had instructions from the pope to arrest Luther if he did not recant. The pope had further instructed Cajetan not to debate with Luther but simply demand that he recant.

Luther was summoned. He traveled to Augsburg convinced he would be arrested and perhaps die a martyr's death. Perhaps he thought he would meet his death like so many others who had protested before him—at the stake amid flames. He had received letters of commendation from Frederick but no safe-conduct from the emperor. Yet he traveled to Augsburg on foot. When he arrived, his clothes showed signs of the journey, and he borrowed a frock in Nuremberg for his audience with the Roman Catholic cardinal. On October 7, 1518, a little less than a year after posting the 95 *Theses,* Luther arrived in Augsburg. The Diet had been adjourned, and most of the princes and court had already departed. The Emperor was still in the area, while the papal legate awaited Luther.

Frederick recommended a few trusted friends stay in Augsburg to watch over Luther, keep him safe, and serve as consultants. In the course of their conversations, they suggested that Luther should not go to Cajetan until he had received an imperial safe-conduct. They were wary of the promises of Cajetan. Even an imperial safe-conduct was not absolute protection. Jan Hus was burned at the stake in Constance (1415) in spite of his safe-conduct from Emperor Sigismund. But it was a prudent step to ask for the safe-conduct, and the emperor was still in the area hunting. For three days Luther resisted the cardinal's invitation to appear before him. Then the safe-conduct arrived from Maximilian's court, and Luther, dressed in his borrowed frock, went to the House of Fugger where Cajetan awaited.

Luther humbly prostrated himself face down on the floor before the feet of Cajetan. He was advised by others on the protocol for such an audience and did not rise until the cardinal invited him to rise. Luther rose to his knees, but the cardinal then invited him to stand. Distinguished Italians and a few of Luther's friends filled the room.

Before the first interview, Luther had learned that he would have no opportunity to dispute or debate the issues before the Roman cardinal. There would be no opportunity to defend either his teachings or his actions. He had been told that he would only have the option of recanting or refusing to recant. Cajetan began the interview in a peaceful and fatherly manner but demanded that Luther recant. Luther had maintained from the beginning that he could not recant unless he was proven to be in error. So he asked the cardinal to explain where he had taught what was wrong.

Cajetan responded by citing two issues. The first was the value of indulgences, and the second was the importance of faith. The cardinal cited papal documents and the teachings of the church to support the papal use of indulgences. Cajetan soon discovered that Luther had thoroughly studied not only the Scriptures but also the papal documents on indulgences. Luther felt that the quotations used by Cajetan lacked sufficient authority to settle the issues he had raised in his *Theses*. In defending his position, Luther cited the Scriptures. The first day of this meeting ended with a disagreement on the absolute and infallible power of the pope to teach what was contrary to the Scriptures. In Luther's view, not only was the sale of indulgences contrary to Scripture, but it was also at variance with the papal documents Cajetan cited. Their interview was a collision of worlds. Cajetan relied on church documents and papal authority to prove his assertions; Luther turned to the Scriptures as the only reliable source of proof and contended that even the pope is not above but under the authority of the Word of God. The divide between them was just as profound on the importance of faith.

In the evening Staupitz arrived in Augsburg to support his monk. The next day Luther came to Cajetan with a written document that supported his protest of the cardinal's thinking. Cajetan dismissed the document, claiming it was idle words. It was clear that the two worlds—Cajetan's and Luther's—had collided and neither could persuade the other. After Luther left, the cardinal summoned Staupitz, hoping that he would be able to convince Luther to recant. It was not to be. Staupitz wondered how he might convince Luther if the distinguished legate from Rome could not. Staupitz, however, did release Luther from his vow of obedience to the Augustinians and suggested a written apology for what Luther had said in the heat of the discussion.

Staupitz and Link, who had been with Luther, left Augsburg thinking that Cajetan might be plotting to arrest them both. Luther remained to finish the letter of apology and wrote another asking Cajetan to receive his appeal to the pope. When Cajetan did not respond for several days, Luther and those still with him grew suspicious. Early in the morning of October 20, Luther suddenly left Augsburg through a little gate in the city wall. He had a wild ride in his knee breeches and stockings on a horse supplied by Staupitz. He returned to Wittenberg on October 30. A year had passed since Luther's invitation to discuss indulgences first hung on the door of the Castle Church. The opposition had not engaged in a debate on the issues Luther raised. Instead they intended to silence him by whatever means necessary and continue the indulgence sales.

An interesting footnote can be added to Luther's discussion with Cajetan. On October 25 Cajetan filed his report to Rome. He realized that Luther was right in claiming that the Roman Church had never officially spoken to clarify the issues related to Tetzel's sale of indulgences. He confessed that Luther should have been allowed to debate the *95 Theses* but concluded that he was a heretic because of what he had said after they were posted. Perhaps Cajetan was thinking of what Luther said at Heidelberg or of his response to Prierias' *Dialogue*. He included in his report an opinion on indulgences, which Leo turned into a papal decree dated November 9, 1518. The document officially confirmed the cardinal's claims about indulgences (Siebert, p. 356). Cajetan wrote to Frederick with his version of the meeting and demanded that the elector turn over the heretic Luther to the Church of Rome.

Luther had come to the conclusion that it was better for him to obey God rather than submit to the Roman Church leaders. He considered indulgences a distortion of the merits of Christ freely offered by God through the gospel. He further concluded that indulgences hid the sure forgiveness of sins based on Christ's merits under a cloud of confusing and distorting words. Later he wrote his own account of the Augsburg interview, on October 31, 1518. In it he would remember that the cardinal "never produced a syllable from the Holy Scriptures against me, and to the present day he could not do so, even if he were to put forth a special effort, since there is universal agreement that nothing is mentioned in the Holy Scriptures about indulgences. On the contrary, the Scriptures commend faith and are as devoid of references to indulgences as they are full of teaching concerning faith" (AE 31, 275-6).

Luther awaited excommunication. He was back in Wittenberg, but he felt he would have to leave because of the papal ban. He appreciated the efforts of Frederick the Wise to keep him in Germany and away from the Roman curia. Nevertheless, Luther was prepared to leave Wittenberg like "Abraham, not knowing where, yet most sure of my way, because God is everywhere," as he wrote Spalatin on November 25, 1518 (AE 48, 94).

Frederick the Wise considered his response to Cajetan's demand of October 25. The faculty of his university endorsed a letter supporting their colleague Luther. They asked that the charges against Luther be spelled out, the reasons given why his position was in error, and then that authorities be cited to support their charges against Luther. That was a request Luther had made from the beginning, but it had never been done. The response of the Roman Church was to silence Luther without due process and condemn him as heretic before any open dialog on the issues. The letter of the faculty, apparently written by Luther himself, was adopted by all. Finally, after a long delay, Frederick responded on December 8. He wrote Cajetan that he would not deliver Luther to the authorities of the church. He cited several reasons: Luther's case had not been thoroughly discussed, he had not been informed in what way he was in error, he had also submitted himself and his case to others for decision, and many learned men were not convinced that Luther was a heretic and unchristian. For the time being, Luther remained in Wittenberg under the protection of Frederick.

Charles von Miltitz Sent to Saxony

Still another attempt to change the elector's mind came from Rome. Charles von Miltitz, a Saxon, was sent to Saxony with the mission of giving Frederick the "golden rose." This was a special honor conferred on a political leader by the papacy. Miltitz was to coordinate his efforts at flattery with Cajetan in order to isolate Luther from the elector and eventually silence him. On the way to Germany, Miltitz discovered that there was widespread support for Luther.

When he arrived, he seems to have acted on his own in seeking to find a diplomatic solution. He met with Luther in early January 1519. While the meeting did not result in Luther's promise to recant, Luther did agree to write a letter of apology to Leo and to remain silent so that the indulgence issue could die quietly. He agreed to the silence as long as his opponents would also remain silent. In addition, Miltitz agreed to persuade the pope to appoint an impartial judge to decide the issue. But the Miltitz mission accomplished little, and it seems his report to Pope Leo gave little more than an optimistic and distorted hope that Luther wanted to comply with Rome's requests.

The end of the protest or the end of opposition to it was not yet in sight. In the next two years another chapter would be written with a new character playing an important role: young Charles V. ❦

NORTH SEA

BALTIC SEA

1500

Feb 24, 1500
Charles born in Ghent, Belgium.

Jan 12, 1519
Emperor Maximilian dies. Young Charles V succeeds his grandfather as emperor.

Wittenberg

London

Ghent

Aachen

ENGLISH CHANNEL

May 2, 1519
Leonardo Da Vinci dies.

Oct 22, 1519
Charles V becomes emperor-elect.

Jan 9, 1522
Adrian VI becomes pope.

ADRIATIC SEA

Sep 14, 1523
Pope Adrian dies.

Nov 19, 1523
Clement VII becomes pope.

Rome

1525

MEDITERRANEAN SEA

CHAPTER FIVE

AACHEN, GERMANY

OCTOBER 22, 1519

hortly after Miltitz' visit with Luther in January 1519, Emperor Maximilian I died, creating a void in the political world of Europe. Most kingdoms in Europe had monarchs born to their positions. France, England, Spain, and the Netherlands were among them. Henry VIII was the heir to the throne of England, and he longed for a male heir to become king after him. Francis I became king of France because he was the eligible heir from the Valois family to become king.

The Netherlands and Spain were the domains of the Hapsburgs, the family of Maximilian. Earlier in his reign, the emperor's son, Philip the Handsome, married Joanna, the daughter of the Spanish king and queen, Ferdinand and Isabella. This marriage tied the Netherlands and Spain (Castile and Aragon) together under the Hapsburg dynasty. Philip was heir apparent, at least until his untimely death. Then Charles was the next in line.

In a story of the Reformation and Luther, this all may seem like pieces of trivial information. But the political landscape of Europe does have much to do with Luther and his protest. Philip, the emperor's son, died suddenly in 1506, leaving his son, Charles, heir to the thrones in the Netherlands and in Spain. Due to the family connections, Charles was not only the grandson of Maximilian but also the grandson of Ferdinand and Isabella of Spain. Because he was only six years old when his father died, Charles could not assume the throne of the Netherlands. His aunt, Margaret, Philip's sister, became regent in the Netherlands. Isabella and Ferdinand still were king and queen of Spain. Charles would have to wait until their deaths to be crowned king of Spain.

Charles was raised in the Netherlands and one of his teachers was Adrian of Utrecht, who had an important influence on Charles. The boy was deeply religious and grew up to be a firm, resolute Roman Catholic. Adrian would later become Pope Adrian VI. His pontificate was short, lasting from January 1522 to September 1523, and came between two significant popes of the Reformation, Leo X and Clement VII.

It is not difficult to understand the deep Roman Catholic faith of Charles. Joanna, his mother, was the daughter of Isabella and Ferdinand. As rulers in Spain, they were designated as Catholic monarchs by Pope Alexander VI in 1496 for defending Catholic dogma within their realms. They defeated the Muslims and united the two kingdoms—Aragon and Castile—to lay the foundation for a united Spain. They also ordered the expulsion of all Jews and Muslims, except those who converted to the Roman Catholic faith. In addition, they instituted the inquisition to purge Spain of everything non-Catholic. We might well remember that they financed the expedition of Christopher Columbus to cross the Atlantic and initiated the Spanish colonization of the new world. Catholic missionaries followed the conquest of the tribes in the new world.

This was the family of Charles. In 1515 he was declared legally of age and assumed the throne of the Netherlands. One year later, at the age of 16, his grandfather, Ferdinand, king of Spain, died, and Charles became king of Spain. He traveled to Spain to assume his new responsibilities in 1517, the year Luther posted his *Theses* on the door of the Castle Church. It was not an easy transition for the new king. Charles confronted difficulties at first from his Spanish subjects. He did not speak Spanish, and the Spaniards were jealous of the influence of his advisors, who were mostly from the Netherlands. At this time his other grandfather, Maximilian, was working to position his grandson to be his successor as emperor of the Holy Roman Empire.

The empire was different from the kingdoms whose rulers received their thrones by right of birth. The emperor was elected. The entire procedure was carefully outlined in a decree of the Imperial Diet at Nuremberg and Metz in 1356. The document setting up the procedure was called the Golden Bull because of the golden seal attached to it. The bull had a noble purpose: to provide an orderly process to select an emperor. Its provision were agreed to in order to avoid struggles and conflict when the emperor died. Seven electors, a kind of electoral college, cast votes to determine the next emperor. The seven included the three spiritual electors of Cologne, Mainz, and Trier and the four secular electors of Bohemia, the Palatinate, Brandenburg, and Saxony. At the time of Luther's first protests, Frederick the Wise of Saxony was one of the electors and therefore a significant factor in the unfolding events of the Reformation.

Maximilian died on January 12, 1519, in Wels, Austria. At his death, three monarchs sought the position of emperor of the Holy Roman Empire—Henry VIII of England, Francis I of France, and Charles. Over the objections of his Spanish advisors, Charles traveled east to promote his candidacy. He and his advisors busily sought the office by influence and money just as the other candidates did.

The papacy and the Roman curia were extremely interested in the outcome. At the time, the pope's interest grew from the uncertainty in how the election of a new emperor would affect the papal states as well as the other states of Italy. Spain had interests in Italy and so did France. The pope, while not directly involved with the election, sought to influence it. The Roman Church's leaders did not want to see the papal states come under the influence of a powerful emperor. Their strategy was to oppose Charles and support the election of Francis. It was a high-stakes political effort for all concerned. Henry VIII soon became an also-ran in the election.

When the pope felt that the candidacy of Francis was in jeopardy, he sought to promote a German candidate in opposition to Charles. He chose Frederick the Wise of Saxony. At the time, Frederick was one of the most respected leaders in Europe. But Frederick did not want to be emperor, in spite of the flattery and bribes of the pope. Perhaps he had had enough imperial politics when he served Maximilian. Eventually the pope abandoned the alternative and embraced the inevitable. A great deal of money was expended by all parties to secure the votes of the seven electors, and the Fuggers loaned money freely. Finally, Charles was elected and became the emperor-elect. He was installed in Aachen on October 22, 1519, according to the provisions of the Golden Bull. In his oath of office, Charles swore to preserve the ancient faith, protect the church, govern justly, and honor the pope. He was emperor-elect with all the power and authority of the crown, but his coronation by the pope would wait for nine years. That event had provided credibility to the office for many earlier emperors.

The territory over which Charles reigned was vast and therefore difficult to rule. A look at the map of the territory of Charles reveals how spread out it was, including Spain, the Netherlands, Germany, and Italy. In addition, it included the Spanish possessions in the new world. France was not part of the empire nor was it part of the territory of the Hapsburgs. France claimed portions of Italy while Charles was heir to other territory in Italy. The complicated family ties of Charles and Francis would eventually bring them into conflict over control of Italy. The dispute that developed would occupy Charles and Francis in a conflict known as the Italian Wars.

At his assumption of the office of emperor-elect in Aachen, the Reformation had already asserted itself in Germany and its influence was growing. To add more trouble to his agenda, the Turks to the east and in the Mediterranean threatened Europe and the empire. Luther, the Germans, the popes—especially Leo X and Clement VII—and Charles became major players in the Reformation history.

Because his empire was so spread out, Charles was often an absent ruler. He designated regents while he was absent, most notably his Aunt Margaret in the Netherlands and later his brother Ferdinand in Germany and Austria, as well as his wife Isabella in Spain. He summoned diets to take care of imperial business. Some of these diets—Worms, Speyer, and Augsburg—had the Reformation on the agenda, but they also included other issues as well. Often one of the most pressing issues was money for military campaigns and other imperial business. The threat of the Turks was a frequent if not an ever-present issue on the emperor's agenda, and during the Italian Wars certainly France and its king consumed time, attention, and money.

When dealing with the challenges in Germany, neither Charles nor his advisors were well acquainted with German, so the language and distance not only created some tension but also meant that his response to issues was often delayed. These factors often hampered his efforts and allowed the problems in Germany to drift along without action. In such an environment it was difficult for Charles to direct his attention to the threat of the Reformation as he intended. He had told the Spanish people when he sailed to seek the German crown that he was concerned about the enemies to the faith. Those enemies he perceived as a threat to peace, the honor of Spain, and the welfare of his kingdom. He was resolved to confront the threat and unite Germany to Spain in one faith, but it became difficult to pursue a concerted effort until the pope crowned him in 1529.

NORTH SEA

BALTIC SEA

1500

1514

Cortez begins conquest of Mexico.

■ Wittenberg

JAN 1, 1519

Zwingli preaches initial sermon at Zurich.

London

Leipzig

ENGLISH CHANNEL

JAN 4-5, 1519

Luther meets with Miltitz in Altenburg.

JUN 27–JUL 6, 1519

Leipzig debate.

JUL 4, 1519

Duke George, fierce opponent of the Reformation, gives permission for Luther to debate Eck.

ADRIATIC SEA

Rome

1525

MEDITERRANEAN SEA

CHAPTER SIX

LEIPZIG, GERMANY

JUNE 27—JULY 16, 1519

he election of an emperor diverted attention away from Luther except perhaps in Germany. After Luther's meeting with von Miltitz in January 1519, he wrote to Frederick that he was willing to "honor the Roman Church in all humility and to place nothing in heaven or on earth above it, save only God himself and his word." If necessary, Luther wrote he was "not only willing to endure the fact that I may never again preach or teach, but I even wish never again to do so" because he was "subordinated to God's command and will." He further proposed "an impartial judge in this case" and nominated the Archbishop of Trier (AE 48, 103-4). In an earlier letter the same month, he had also agreed "to issue a little book to admonish everyone to follow the Roman Church, to be obedient and respect it, and to understand my writings as having been intended to bring not dishonor but honor to the holy Roman church" (AE 48, 98). Luther continued to maintain that he would recant if he could be proven wrong on the basis of the Scriptures or on evidence from church history.

Frederick the Wise continued to look for a way to preserve the integrity of his university in Wittenberg and its most prominent professor. He was convinced that a fair and impartial trial for Luther was his best course of action. As a senior and respected political leader in the empire, his words carried much weight. The mission of Charles von Miltitz to Saxony gave testimony to his political importance.

One of the agreements that came from the meeting Luther had with von Miltitz was that Luther would remain silent as long as those who opposed him also remained silent. While the drama of international politics with the election of a new emperor unfolded, the curtain rose on another act in the drama of Luther's protest. John Eck sought an opportunity to confront and discredit Luther. He had befriended Luther at Augsburg but later attacked his teachings. At that time Luther responded but sought to repair the friendship.

Eck Challenges Luther's Assertions

Eck, on the other hand, renewed his opposition to Luther by calling for a debate, but not with Luther. After all, Luther had already been declared a heretic. So Eck challenged a Wittenberg colleague of Luther—Andreas Carlstadt. Luther and everyone else understood that Eck's real target was Luther and his teachings. Leipzig was to be the site of the debate. Because the debate was with Carlstadt, the rules of the debate prevented Luther from entering the debate without permission. Yet he prepared for it by studying and by seeking permission to participate from Duke George of Saxony, who, with the University of Leipzig, was the sponsor of the debate.

As expected, the articles for the debate published by Eck focused on issues that targeted Luther more than Carlstadt. One of the issues took the conflict between Luther and Rome to a new level. Eck challenged what Luther had said about the origin and primacy of the papacy after the posting of the *95 Theses*. Luther had claimed that the Roman bishop had not ruled over the Greek church for many of the early centuries after Christ and that at least part of the Christian church therefore had existed outside the authority of Rome. When Eck asserted that whoever succeeded Peter had always been the primary bishop and Vicar of Christ, Luther responded. He wrote that the "decrees of the Roman pontiffs which have appeared in the last four hundred years" were "feeble" in their claim "that the Roman church is superior to all others." Luther maintained that "against them stand the history of eleven hundred years, the test of divine Scripture, and the decree of the Council of Nicaea, the most sacred of all councils" (AE 31, 318).

So where was the discussion of the indulgences? Under the surface of the *95 Theses*, the real issue was papal authority. Whether the pope was infallible and could make doctrine beyond Scripture was a profound and pivotal issue. Luther had challenged the assumption of the papal claims concerning indulgences. That was the issue between Luther and Cajetan in Augsburg. The Roman cardinal supported indulgences by quoting earlier papal decrees and later drafted a document that Leo issued to clarify indulgence practices. But even before the clarification by Leo, it was a matter of Rome's authority. Leo instructed Cajetan not to debate Luther but only to require his obedience to Rome and recant his position. From the Roman perspective, the sale of indulgences was assumed to be correct because the pope said so and the later teachers of the church agreed. Luther did not agree with Rome's claim and objected to the citations that supported the practice. He criticized Cajetan because Cajetan did not quote one word of Scripture to prove the use of indulgences and cited no references to them in the writings of the early church fathers. A year and a half after October 31, 1517, Luther's objection to the abuses in the sale of indulgences crystalized into the issue of authority—Rome's pronouncements or the Bible and which one should be followed when they were opposed to each other.

While waiting for the debate in Leipzig, Luther prepared but did not receive permission to participate before he left Wittenberg with Carlstadt and others. When they arrived, he sat among the spectators for the opening sessions of the debate on June 27, 1519. The first phase of the debate between Eck and Carlstadt turned out not to be as one-sided as imagined. Eck was a talented debater with expectations to quickly dispatch his opponent. Carlstadt in his plodding and methodical way was no match for the energetic and polished Eck, but Carlstadt often proved his points clearly and convincingly. Yet Eck claimed victory and was ready to advance to the next level—debate with Luther. Duke George finally granted permission for Luther to participate.

The main event between Luther and Eck in Leipzig began on July 4 and ended after two weeks of arguments and counter arguments. Eck had maintained the traditional belief in the primacy of Rome. Luther had countered with arguments from the Scriptures. Luther maintained that when Christ said, "You are Peter. And on this rock I will build my church" (Matthew 16:18), he was referring not to Peter himself but to Peter's confession of faith. This was a concept that earlier church fathers had maintained and was based on the Greek words used by Matthew. Luther went on to support his thought by citing passages that said only Christ is the foundation of the church (1 Corinthians 3:11 and 1 Peter 2:4,5). In addition, Luther claimed that the early church and the Eastern church never acknowledged the divine origin or supremacy of the Roman bishop.

Eck countered and suggested that Luther had adopted some of the teachings of Jan Hus, who had been condemned as a heretic and burned at the stake by the Council of Constance. Luther objected to his tactic as irrelevant to the issue of the debate but also suggested that not all of Hus's thoughts were heretical. At this point, Duke George shook his head, put his hands to his side, and said loudly enough for others to hear, "May the plague take him." Luther's assertion on Hus had created an enemy.

The outcome of the debate was to be decided by the faculties of two important universities—the University of Paris and the University of Erfurt. The decision from Paris was long in coming. It finally appeared just before Luther appeared before the Imperial Diet of Worms in 1521. The decision from Erfurt never came; the faculty chose not to respond. Two other universities—Louvain and Cologne—did respond. Both concluded that Eck had bested Luther, but they based their opinions not so much on the debate but on a collection of Luther's works that had begun to circulate throughout Europe.

After the debate and before the judgment of Louvain, Cologne, or Paris, Eck enjoyed the apparent victory and basked in the rise of his reputation. Luther was disappointed after the debate. In a letter to Spalatin, he used the word *tragedy* to refer to the events in Leipzig (AE 31, 325). Luther made enemies and lost friends because of the debate; Eck had maneuvered him to speak well of some of the teachings of Jan Hus who had been condemned 100 years earlier. But the debate also advanced Luther's reputation. Enrollment at Wittenberg grew rapidly after the debate. Some considered Luther the tip of the spear resisting Rome. He deserved their support for his efforts to reform the church. As a result, many rallied to his support. And the collection of Luther's works that was being circulated so widely had just the opposite of turning them against him. In fact, Luther's works won many to the side of his protest against Rome. ❦

1520

JUN 24, 1520

Pope Leo X issues papal bull excommunicating Luther.

1520

Luther publishes key Reformation treatises.

Jun: *Treatise on Good Works*

Aug: *To the Christian Nobility*

Oct: *The Babylonian Captivity of the Church*

Nov: *On the Freedom of a Christian*

SEP 30, 1520

Suleiman becomes sultan of Turkey.

DEC 10, 1520

Luther burns the papal bull. Pope Leo excommunicates Luther.

1521

NORTH SEA

BALTIC SEA

Wittenberg

London

ENGLISH CHANNEL

ADRIATIC SEA

Rome

MEDITERRANEAN SEA

CHAPTER SEVEN

WITTENBERG, GERMANY

DECEMBER 10, 1520

he "tragedy" of the Leipzig debate can also be viewed as a tragic step away from any real reformation of abuses. The temporary truce of rhetoric was broken on both sides. The election of a new emperor even became secondary news. Once the dust had settled from the political stage and Charles V was emperor of the Holy Roman Empire, the focus shifted once more to the German problem—Martin Luther. In November 1519, Leo X asked Eck to come to Rome to report. His report troubled the pope. Miltitz was once more sent to Germany to impress upon Frederick the Wise the consequences of protecting Luther. But Frederick remained steady in his desire to have Luther's case brought before an unbiased court on German soil.

For the church, Leipzig was indeed a step away from the wide reformation many desired and a step toward the status quo in Rome and Europe. Most believed that Eck had won and that with his victory Rome had won. But it was a step that still could be retraced. In Luther's early commentary on Galatians, he asserted that the pope might still be the supreme pontiff, but "it would be most impious to attribute to him in addition virtue and wisdom equal to the virtue and wisdom of Christ" (AE 27, 156). He also distinguished between the Roman Church and the Roman curia. The Roman Church he asserted was "the bride of Christ, the daughter of God, the terror of hell, the victory over the flesh", but the curia "is known by its fruits" (158). Hope for a united but reformed church still survived. But in just a short year, by the end of 1520, only confrontation remained.

After Leipzig, Luther returned to Wittenberg to resume his duties at the university. The first edition of his commentary on Galatians came off the press in September of 1519. Luther had been working on the commentary since 1516. His appreciation for the gospel grew from his tower discovery—an understanding that righteousness is a gift of God for the sake of Christ to unworthy sinners who possess it by faith. Luther held to this concept and grew in understanding its implications. Because he grasped its importance, he hazarded all to maintain it. He could not keep silent about the treasure of the gospel, especially when others opposed it. In the 1519 edition of Galatians he declared, "Only let me not be found guilty of impious silence" (AE 27, 159).

For himself, Luther felt that it was necessary "to flee for refuge to the most solid rock of Divine Scripture and not to believe rashly any, whoever they may be, who speak, decide, or act contrary to its authority" (AE 27, 156). He often cited 1 Thessalonians 5:21: "Test everything. Hold on to the good" and practiced the principle in his research of church documents, testing everything against the standard of the Bible. He wished his enemies would follow the same principle, but they did not. Instead they turned to the authority of the pope and the decrees and documents of the church.

Luther's Important Writings in 1520

Luther was often brash and vehement. Much of the time, his writings flowed from his pen in the heat of controversy. The effort of battle often made him intemperate. The hungry printing press gobbled up his words sometimes, it seemed, even before the ink on Luther's page was dry. An equally hungry audience consumed the latest tract or book even when the language was vehement and harsh. The content and ideas were vital. But not all his writing was so abrasive. He continued to write after Leipzig and produced several important works. Four of them require our attention. Each of them added a profound insight to Luther's protest and deepened the division between the protester and the curia.

The first of them, *Treatise on Good Works* (AE 44, 15-114), is not harsh, abrasive, or vehement. Spalatin, Luther's friend and the private secretary of Frederick, suggested that he write on the subject. The teaching of justification by faith alone (by grace alone) without human works was the keystone for Luther. But for many, that central issue seemed to lead to a total neglect of good works. They feared Luther's emphasis on justification without works would lead to the rise of lawlessness and immorality. After some hesitation and then in a calm and pastoral way, Luther took up the task and explained the importance of good works for the Christian. His vision of good works based on the Scriptures placed good works in a context completely different from the teachings of the Roman Church. Philip Melanchthon, Luther's colleague and co-reformer, said that this treatise was Luther's best writing on faith and good works.

The *Treatise on Good Works* is built around the Ten Commandments. The Commandments are the standard for a Christian's good works. Luther wrote, "There are no good works except those works God has commanded, just as there is no sin except that which God has forbidden" (AE 44, 23). The Scriptures also taught Luther the importance of faith. Luther commented, "The first, highest, and most precious of all good works is faith in Christ" (23) and that faith was active in a Christian's life. "Now faith is the master workman and the motivating force behind the good works. . . . apart from faith all works are dead, no matter how wonderful they look or what splendid names they have" (109, 113).

But that seemed so different from the traditional way of considering good works. For most, works were done to earn a reward (called *satisfaction*), less time in purgatory, and even heaven. Faith simply received the free gift of God's forgiveness and with it eternal life and salvation. If the "reward" was already given away to sinners freely by grace, for many that seemed to destroy the motivation to do any good work. But what Luther said on the basis of the Scriptures was different. Instead, the Christian heart receives forgiveness, freely given by God before any human effort. Then the heart is healed so it can serve God and others with good works. Luther wrote, "A Christian man who lives in this confidence toward God (that he is forgiven freely) knows all things, can do all things, ventures everything that needs to be done, and does everything gladly and willingly, not that he may gather merits and good works, but because it is a pleasure for him to please God in doing these things. He simply serves God with no thought of reward, content that his service pleases God" (27). In another place where Luther commented on the Seventh Commandment in regard to greed and generosity, he wrote, "If the heart expects and puts its trust in divine favor, how can a man be greedy and anxious? Such a man is absolutely certain that he is acceptable to God: therefore, he does not cling to money; he uses his money cheerfully and freely for the benefit of his neighbor" (108).

Luther certainly could not see the future, but as he considered the importance of faith in the free gift of God's grace in Christ, he anticipated the conflict ahead. Written in March 1520, this might be a commentary on Luther's stand before the emperor at the Diet of Worms a year later in 1521: "For where there is such faith and confidence there is also a bold, defiant, fearless heart that risks all and stands by the truth, no matter what the cost, whether it is against pope or king, as we see that the dear martyrs did. For such a heart is satisfied and serenely sure that it has a gracious, kindly-disposed God. Therefore, he despises all the favors, grace, goods, and honor of men, and does not attach any value to these transitory things" (112).

As pastoral and positive as the *Treatise on Good Works* was, problems with the abuses in the church of his day were not far from his mind. Earlier Luther had hoped that a general council would correct the abuses, but now he wrote, "We have had many councils . . . such as Constance, Basel, and the last Lateran council. Nothing came of these councils and things are going from bad to worse" (91). His hope for reform no longer rested in a council under the control of the pope and curia.

The second important treatise was titled *To the Christian Nobility of the German Nation Concerning the Reform of the Christian Estate,* commonly referred to simply as *To the Christian Nobility* (AE 44, 123-217). It marked out a different direction for reform. In this treatise, written during the summer 1520, Luther addressed the princes in the hope of challenging them to reform the church. Many sincere Roman Catholic Christians still looked for the reforms that the recent councils had failed to accomplish. Those who opposed Luther asserted the absolute power of the pope after the Leipzig debate just as they had done before. Luther responded. The issue remained "the reform of the Christian estate" (123). He addressed the new emperor, Charles V, reminding him and the other secular rulers that "Often the councils have made some pretense at reformation, but their attempts have been cleverly frustrated. . . . God has given us a young man of noble birth as head of state, and in him has awakened great hopes of good in many hearts. Presented with such an opportunity we ought to apply ourselves and use this time of grace profitably" (124-5).

This call to action was based on the principle that every Christian was equal before God and possessed the same spiritual blessings. When Luther claimed that every Christian is a priest by Baptism, he gave voice to what we have come to call the priesthood of all believers. Because each one was equal before God, each one therefore had the duty and right to oppose and correct abuses in society and the church.

With this teaching, Luther removed the special distinction the ordained clergy had over the laity. Ministry or service to God's people is the only distinction that sets anyone apart from other Christians, not ordination or holy orders. The Roman clergy claimed superiority by virtue of ordination and even claimed to be above all temporal (civil) powers. Luther asserted that the church had no temporal power greater than the princes, and the church was even subject to the temporal power in all things except spiritual matters. This was a concept that had been lost. For centuries the pope's claim of temporal power was based on a document called the *Donation of Constantine.* This document claimed that Constantine gave the bishop of Rome temporal power in the West. Laurentius Valla in 1440, however, proved it to be a forgery. Luther had seen Valla's work just before he wrote this treatise. But there was more than just the revelation of the forgery to Luther's treatise. He further challenged the pope's right to exclusive interpretation of the Scriptures and the pope's claim that he is the only one who has the authority to call or confirm a council. He asserted that such authority was presumptuous and that "no Christian authority can do anything against Christ" (138). The treatise concluded with 27 issues that needed to be corrected.

The treatise also moved forward onto the fertile ground of a growing sense of German nationalism. He wrote, "Above all, we should drive out of German territory the papal legates with their faculties, which they sell to us for large sums of money" (193). Luther did not write this treatise in isolation. Instead he collaborated with members of the Saxon court and others. It became a sensation in Germany. The first printing of 4,000 copies was gone in two weeks. Some believed his thoughts were rash. Luther himself said, "I know full well that I have been very outspoken. I have made many suggestions that will be considered impractical. I have attacked many things too severely. But how else ought I to do it? I am duty-bound to speak" (216-7).

The third tract was still more outspoken and severe. The title itself was antagonistic and raised a sharp battle cry against the Roman curia: *The Babylonian Captivity of the Church* (AE 36, 11-126). Yet Luther was not a careless, enraged bull smashing everything without careful study. Luther's opponents, such as Prierias and Eck, drove him to study the Scriptures, the papal decrees, and church history. *The Babylonian Captivity* treatise was written in Latin for scholars, while the treatise *To the German Nobility* was written in German for the Germans of noble and common rank.

The Babylonian Captivity took aim at the sacramental system of the Roman Catholic Church at the time. Luther claimed that the seven sacraments of the church had no justification in the Scriptures or in the history of the early church. This return to what the Bible revealed is an often-repeated theme for Luther. He wanted to restore Christianity to its roots and clear away what had been added to the church's doctrine and practice and violated the teachings of the apostles. What Luther saw in the seven sacraments at the time were practices that had been added by human effort, thought, and decree. Their existence was not evident in the Scriptures or the early church, and the creation of them had enslaved Christians and made them subject to human rather than divine thought. The primacy of the pope was at issue here as in other writings. Could the pope make doctrine not contained in the Scriptures? Luther said no; his opponents had been saying yes ever since Luther invited discussion about the abuses of indulgences.

Luther maintained that the Scriptures taught that Holy Communion was to be offered in both kinds—bread and wine—contrary to the practice of the Roman Catholic Church. The Roman Church, he claimed, had altered Christ's institution of the Sacrament. Withholding the wine and thereby distorting the Sacrament was a serious overextension of human authority. Luther wrote, "If we permit one institution of Christ to be changed, we make all of his laws invalid, and any man may make bold to say that he is not bound by any other law or institution of Christ" (21). What was decisive for Luther was what Christ said on Maundy Thursday and not what popes and scholars said after that.

It was a bold assertion and a fundamental attack on the power of the church to change such sacred things as the Sacraments. The priests did not have the power to forbid God's people to receive both kinds—bread and wine—or change the bread and wine into the body and blood of Christ. Nor is the Sacrament or Mass an additional sacrifice for sin offered to God. It is instead, as Christ instituted it, the gift and promise of the full forgiveness gained when Christ gave his body and blood for the remission of sins. On the issue of transubstantiation—the papal doctrine of Christ's presence in the Sacrament—Luther wrote, "The church kept the true faith for more than twelve hundred years, during which time the holy fathers never, at any time or place, mentioned this transubstantiation" (31).

For Luther, only Baptism and the Lord's Supper carried New Testament authority. Penance, although it had the same authority and announced forgiveness, had been corrupted and had no visible earthly component. Marriage—even if instituted by God—along with confirmation, holy orders, and last rites, may be important, but they do not rise to the level of sacrament. Marriage had no visible element like Baptism and Holy Communion. Confirmation, ordination, and last rites were church rites that were perhaps even profitable for the church, but they lacked Christ's institution. Luther observed, "Neither pope nor bishop nor any other man has the right to impose a single syllable of law upon a Christian man without his consent" (70).

A Gentle Work of Great Importance

On January 9, 1520, the Roman curia officially reopened the case against Luther, who they put under suspicion of heresy. Cardinal Cajetan was the co-chair of the commission. Later that year in May or June, John Eck went to Rome to join the commission and share his insight. Finally on June 24, 1520, a papal bull was published in Rome that gave Luther 60 days to recant once the bull was posted in Germany. The bull was called *Exsurge Domine* (Arise O Lord) and cited 41 articles from Luther's writings that were condemned. John Eck and Aleander, the secretary of the Vice-Chancellor of the Roman curia, were sent north on July 18 with the authority to publish the bull and execute its decree to excommunicate Luther if he did not recant within 60 days. Their mission included the authority to publicly burn Luther's books.

With the papal bull on its way north, Charles von Miltitz reappeared, hoping to achieve some kind of last-minute reconciliation. He met with Luther on October 12, 1520. At that meeting Luther agreed to write a conciliatory letter to Pope Leo X and add a brief booklet. The result was another significant book from the pen of Luther: *The Freedom of a Christian* (AE 31, 333-77). It was not antagonistic, like *The Babylonian Captivity of the Church,* but rather calm, much in the tone of his *Treatise on Good Works* earlier in the year. Luther, true to his promise, wrote in his dedication to Leo X, "I am sending you this little treatise dedicated to you as a token of peace and good hope. . . . It is a small book if you regard its size. Unless I am mistaken, however, it contains the whole of Christian life in a brief form" (343). At this point in the unfolding events, it was a gesture without effect. The decision was already made in Rome to excommunicate Luther and, in Wittenberg, the protester had decided to oppose Rome and die for his faith and teaching if necessary.

Yet *The Freedom of a Christian* has a deeper significance than the coming excommunication of Luther. Three years earlier, Luther protested the abuses of Tetzel's efforts to sell indulgences. Luther spent a great deal of time and energy in research of Roman Catholic documents before posting them. His *Theses* aroused vehement opposition. The criticism pushed him to continue his research. The protest against indulgences evolved into questions of reform and papal authority. Again Luther was driven to think and sharpen his vision. What now emerged was not a protest against church practice, politics, or policy. It was a fundamental difference with the teachings of the Roman Catholic Church. *The Freedom of a Christian* together with *The Treatise on Good Works, The Babylonian Captivity,* and *To the German Nobility* articulated this deep division. It was a matter of doctrine and teaching and the source of authority for those teachings—Scripture or the papacy.

The Freedom of a Christian asserted two apparently contradictory ideas: "A Christian is a perfectly free lord of all subject to none" and "A Christian is a perfectly dutiful servant of all, subject to all." The key to the first is justification by faith. "Faith alone, without works, justifies, frees, and saves" (348). Because of this justification, "Every Christian is by faith so exalted above all things that, by virtue of a spiritual power, he is lord of all things without exception, so that nothing can do him any harm" (354). The reason a Christian does works is not to earn righteousness or obtain salvation, "but he does the works out of spontaneous love in obedience to God and considers nothing except the approval of God" (359).

The key to the second principle is love. Luther wrote, "Faith is truly active through love, that is, it finds expression in works of the freest service, cheerfully and lovingly done, with which a man willingly serves another without hope of reward" (365). Faith is not a sterile academic exercise, but faith in the free justification from sin by faith on account of Christ subjects us to love and serve others. Luther stated further, "We conclude, therefore, that a Christian lives not in himself, but in Christ and in his neighbor. Otherwise he is not a Christian. He lives in Christ through faith, in his neighbor through love. By faith he is caught up beyond himself into God. By love he descends beneath himself into his neighbor" (371). "Our faith in Christ does not free us from works but from false opinions concerning works, that is, from the foolish presumption that justification is acquired by works" (372,373). What Luther discovered in the Tower Experience earlier is clearly now at the center of his protest. We do not achieve righteousness through our efforts in this life or our suffering in purgatory in the next. Righteousness is God's gift to us through faith in Christ. Faith alone justifies, but faith is never alone, never without actions of obedience to God and love for others.

The crack that had shown itself between Luther and Cajetan in Augsburg grew wider. It was now a deep chasm that defied solution. Eck and Aleander, the papal representatives, published the papal bull of excommunication. They confiscated Luther's books and burned them in Ingolstadt, the home of John Eck, and in Mainz, Louvain, and Cologne. But they encountered opposition in Leipzig, Torgau, and Erfurt, where Luther's reforms were gaining traction.

Of course, Luther had received a copy of the papal bull and knew of the bonfires around Europe that consumed his books. On December 10, 1520, in Wittenberg, Luther's colleague, Philip Melanchthon, posted an announcement on the university bulletin board. In that announcement he invited the student body to assemble outside the east gate of the city. A pile of wood occupied the spot in preparation for a book burning. The books designated for the fire, however, supported the teaching of the Roman curia. Primary among those books was a set of Canon Law that gave the pope the authority Luther had opposed. While they warmed themselves in the heat of the fire, Luther tossed a copy of the papal bull *Exsurge Domine* into the fire. As it burned, any bridge to reconciliation with Rome also burned. ❦

1520

JAN 28, 1521

Charles convenes Diet at Worms.

APR 16, 1521

Luther arrives in Worms. Charles V convened the Diet of Worms and summoned Luther to attend.

APR 18, 1521

Luther responds, "Here I Stand."

APR 22, 1521

French King Francis I declares war on Spain.

APR 26, 1521

Luther leaves Worms.

APR 27, 1521

Magellan killed in Philippines.

MAY 26, 1521

Edict of Worms published condemning Luther and his followers.

1525

CHAPTER EIGHT

WORMS, GERMANY

APRIL 18, 1521

Much history was yet to be played out in Germany, Rome, and several battlefields in Europe. Yet Luther had sounded a dramatic note. He had burned the last papal bull to be issued to a united Western church. From this point on, confrontation and conflict would be part of the history. Attempts at compromise would occur, a truce would surface here and there, but the impasse would remain and reassert itself.

Luther's protest had challenged the status quo. At first, the Roman curia and Leo X assumed that the assertion of papal power and authority would be enough to silence the German monk, whom they greatly underestimated. When Cajetan came to Augsburg to assert Rome's authority and demand Luther to recant, he may have been surprised at the depth of Luther's research. Luther was unwilling to accept papal claims because his research had clearly demonstrated that popes and councils had in the past contradicted each other. Luther was frustrated that Cajetan opposed him simply because popes in recent history had decreed indulgences were official doctrine. Luther wanted a more reliable basis for Christian teaching and practice. He turned to and appealed to the Scriptures as the base for it.

But Rome did not agree. The responses that came from Rome after Luther's interview in Augsburg maintained the same hard line of papal authority. The difference was clear in Leipzig. In the course of the debate, Luther honestly reflected on the 400 years of history before the debate. He asserted that the papacy as it had come to be known in 1520 was not the same as it had been only 400 years earlier. And the church was certainly much different than the early Christian church before and after the Council of Nicea in 325. The idea of an inconsistent and contradictory authority was unacceptable to

Luther. No one engaged him on the basis of historical research into the apostolic church, the church of the early church fathers, or on the basis of the Scriptures. The objections from the Roman Catholic faithful had driven him to question his conclusions, do more research, and then grow more confident and defiant. Finally, the 41 heresies cited in the pope's bull, *Exsurge Domine,* were supported not on the basis of Scripture but on what the Roman Church had taught and decreed. Luther grew firmer in his protest.

In addition, his protest continued to grow legs and spread. The church longed for reform. The reform councils of a previous generation had failed to reform the church. The councils merely succeeded in bringing an end to the papal schism. Two popes—one from Rome and one from Avignon—no longer vied for control of the church. But the indulgence trade of Tetzel in Germany became a symptom of the disease and a demonstration for the need of reform. The church was focused more on temporal power and prestige than on the gospel. It was more concerned about its authority and revenue than the care of souls and the truth God had revealed to the ancient church in the Scriptures. The protest of a single monk in Germany had found eager supporters not only in Germany but also in other parts of Europe. His works were smuggled into England and Italy, hidden in shipments of goods. In Italy, German traders secretly read Luther's works. When the Edict of Worms required Luther's works to be burned, those works found the flames not only in Germany but also in many other countries in northern Europe. They were also thrown into the fire in England. In 1527 they were even publicly burned at the Rialto Bridge in Venice. It is difficult to underestimate the spread of Luther's thought.

From Rome's perspective, something had to be done to assert the old order and stifle the voices of protest. But it seemed to require more than papal authority. Luther defied the papacy and publicly burned its bull. The next step was an alliance between the papacy and the emperor—Charles V. As a 20-year-old he had become emperor in 1520. At first it looked like peace would reign among the nations with the ascent of the new emperor. Francis I, king of France, and Henry VIII, king of England, met in northern France in a lavish show of friendship called the Field of the Golden Cloth. It was so called because the fabric of the tents was woven with threads of gold. Splendor and courtly etiquette seemed to announce a time of accord. Charles V was only a short distance away in Calais.

But significant differences would soon arise. The pope was not so confident of the peace and concord that seemed so evident. He may have even been worried about the growing power of Charles and what that would mean to Italy and the papal states. For that reason and others, he had supported the candidacy of Francis for emperor. When Francis was not a viable candidate, he had also suggested Frederick the Wise. That was all in the past now, and Leo X accepted the inevitable choice of Charles V. New negotiations and new alliances would have to achieve his ends. What would unfold would be a political power struggle of alliances, counter-alliances, and armies on the battlefields of Europe.

Charles Summons a Diet in Worms

Soon Charles had to address the challenges of being emperor. One of the issues involved the persistent protests of Luther. The presses continued to offer what this German rebel wrote, and Europe was eager for each new publication. Rome expected Charles simply to ratify the papal bull against Luther, but it was not that simple. In this situation, Charles had to confront a difficult reality. He needed money for a campaign against the Turks. The source of revenue included his newly acquired German Empire. So, solving the question of Luther's protest involved the Germans. When Charles became emperor, he promised not to condemn any German without first giving him an impartial hearing in Germany. At the beginning of his reign, the new emperor had to balance political and spiritual concerns. His approach was to summon everyone to a diet in Worms, Germany.

Just before the Diet of Worms was convened, Luther wrote to his friend John Staupitz, who had been the head of the Augustinians when Luther first began to have questions. Staupitz was concerned about what lay ahead for Luther. Both knew that something serious was at hand. Luther reminded his former superior how Staupitz had counseled the young monk at the beginning: "Most Reverend Father, you said to me among other things, 'Remember, Friar, you began this in the name of our Lord Jesus Christ.' I have accepted this word not as coming from you but as spoken to me through you, and I have kept it firmly in mind ever since" (AE 48, 191). In the same letter Luther also wondered how things might have been different if the pope "had begun this affair with good mediators for establishing peace rather than with force and storms for the destruction of Luther" (192). But it had not been. Luther was given only one choice from Roman Catholic officials: recant. So it was in Augsburg and so it would also be in Worms in spite of Luther's hope for a fair hearing.

Luther was happy that the emperor would take up his case. He wrote to Frederick 11 days after his letter to Staupitz, "I heartily rejoice that His Imperial Majesty wants to take upon himself this case; God willing, it is a case of

God, of universal Christendom, and of the whole German nation—and not of a single man, much less my own" (195). Luther wanted his case to "be turned over to devout, learned, understanding, trustworthy, and Christian men, both clergymen and laymen, who are well versed in the Bible and who understand and differentiate between divine and human laws and commands, in order to discuss the case carefully with me" (196).

Frederick the Wise became a principle player in the history that unfolded in Worms. After the bull of excommunication was issued, Frederick refused to turn over Luther in spite of all the pressure from Rome. He insisted that since Luther had appealed his case from Roman jurisdiction to the emperor, he would remain free until the results of that appeal were known. Charles, for many reasons, agreed when he summoned the Imperial Diet at Worms. It convened on January 28, 1521.

Aleander represented the pope in Worms and sought to convince the emperor to take strong and decisive action against Luther. Frederick took an equally strong position against Aleander. The compromise resulted in Luther's summons to Worms with the assurance of an imperial safe-conduct. The summons arrived in Wittenberg on March 26. Shortly after receiving the summons, Luther and others left Wittenberg for Worms.

One significant development occurred that seemed unrelated to Luther at the time but would signal later events that would influence Charles and the course of Luther's protest. Military forces opposed to Charles invaded the Netherlands. The invasion was contrary to all existing treaties, and many suspected that France was behind it. Francis I expressed his deep desire for peace, claimed he was not the aggressor, and insisted he was innocent of any involvement. However, later an intercepted letter made it clear that France was indeed giving aid to those responsible for the invasion. The Imperial Diet of Worms had a new agenda item—an imperial response to the invasion of the emperor's territory. The conflict between Charles and Francis had begun.

Luther's First Appearance Before the Diet

Meanwhile in Germany, Luther and his small party made their way to Worms. Many of his friends had advised him not to go. They believed that the safe-conduct issued by Charles would be no better than the safe-conduct offered by Emperor Sigismund to Jan Hus. In spite of Sigismund's safe-conduct, Hus was imprisoned and eventually burned at the stake. Luther was nevertheless determined to go. Along the way Luther learned that Charles had already issued a condemnation against him before his appearance in Worms—another reason for his friends to suggest that Luther refuse to comply with the imperial summons. But Luther remained steadfast. He wrote to Spalatin, "Of course I realize that the mandate of Charles has also been published to frighten me. But Christ lives, and we shall enter Worms in spite of all the gates of hell and the powers of the air" (198).

In some cities on the trip to Worms, Luther received a cool reception. In others, a very warm one. Many wanted to see Luther, perhaps thinking they would not see him again. At times he preached to large crowds along the way. After two weeks of travel, on April 16 at about 10 o'clock in the morning, a trumpet announced his arrival in Worms. He was escorted into the city by a band of knights who had ridden out to meet him. A large crowd—some estimate it at 2,000—hailed Luther in the streets of Worms. All wanted to see Luther. Aleander, the pope's representative and only eye witness to record Luther's arrival, said that when Luther stepped down from his wagon, one priest embraced him and touched his monastic gown three times. Luther said, "God will be with me." The reformer from Saxony was a celebrity. That evening he was greeted by some of the princes. The next step was up to Charles and his counselors.

Just before 4:00 in the afternoon of the next day, April 17, Luther was summoned to appear before the Diet. The crowds were still straining for a glimpse of Luther. His escort, the imperial marshal, had to lead Luther through side streets and even through the gardens and passages of private homes. Finally, Luther made his way through the crowds that filled the entrance to the hall. As he approached the doors, they swung open and he stepped into the hall.

Luther surveyed an impressive assembly. Charles V, who sat before him, was officially known with all dignity as "Roman King; future Emperor; *sempter augustus;* King of Spain, Sicily, Jerusalem, the Balearic Islands, the Canary Islands, the Indies, and the mainland on the far side of the Atlantic; Archduke of Austria; Duke of Burgundy, Brabant, Styria, Carinthia, Carniola, Luxemburg, Limburg, Athens, and Patras; Count of Hapsburg, Flanders, and Tyrol; Count Palatine of Burgundy, Hainault, Pfirt, Roussilon, and Landgrave of Alsace; Count of Swabia; and Lord of Asia and Africa" (Brandi 113). His brother, Archduke Ferdinand, along with 6 electors, 24 dukes, and many other dignitaries, filled out the 204 people present in the hall. The marshal advised Luther to say nothing until he was addressed.

Luther waited silently. Dr. John Eck—not the same John Eck who debated Luther at Leipzig—in a loud and clear voice posed two questions for Luther, first in Latin and then in German. The Diet wanted to know whether he wrote the assembled books (about 20) on a table before him. The second question was whether Luther would retract them and recant. Luther's advocate, who accompanied him, asked that the titles be read. The titles included some devotional materials such as Luther's exposition of the Lord's Prayer and Psalms, as well as some of his more controversial works.

After the titles were read, Luther acknowledged in both Latin and German that the titles were his work. He spoke in a low and soft tone. The second question was more difficult to answer because Luther's answer would determine his fate. He was ready to die just as Jan Hus had 100 years before. Then, unexpectedly, Luther calmly asked for 24 hours to consider his response to the second question. The emperor, after a consultation with his advisors, granted Luther's request. Luther's delay confirmed the opinion of those who thought he was a fool.

Luther's Second Appearance Before the Diet

Luther was escorted back to his lodgings for the evening. That night was spent in prayer and steeling his resolve. He wrote a brief report to John Cuspinian: "I appeared at this hour before the Emperor and the Imperial diet. I was questioned as to whether I would want to renounce my books. I answered then that these were certainly my books and that I would tell them my opinion concerning any renunciation the following day, since more opportunity and time for deliberation on this issue has been neither asked nor granted. *[Luther thought he might be asked some questions to clarify his work and was not advised in advance he would be asked only two questions.]* With Christ's help, however, I shall not in all eternity recant the least particle" (AE 48, 200).

The next day Luther was summoned to the hall again at 4 o'clock in the afternoon, but he did not immediately enter. He waited two hours before he was brought before the Diet to give his answer. The candles and torches lit the hall, and Luther stood before the assembled Diet as John Eck again repeated the two questions.

In Luther's first response to the second question, he divided the books on the table into three classes. First, he said some books presented universal Christian truths. Even his enemies could find nothing in them to retract. Second, he admitted to writing books that criticized the papacy. These works were a protest to the false teachings of the Roman Church and the scandalous lives of her leaders at the time. If he withdrew these writings, Luther asserted, it would only encourage the abuses and those responsible for them. His protest was to check those abuses. Third, some of the books were against individuals who defended the papacy. He admitted that he might have attacked them with too much animosity and hostility, but he could not retract those writings because it would sanction the errors that those writers defended as well as the acrimony of his adversaries. He concluded that he would retract every error only if he could be convinced of his errors from the writings of the prophets and apostles.

Luther had spoken in German with so much modesty and firmness that Elector Frederick was deeply impressed. Then Luther was asked to repeat his answer in Latin. When he was finished, he was challenged again by Eck, who claimed that he had not answered the question. He asked Luther to give a clear and precise answer "without horns or any evasion." Luther responded, "Since your Majesty and your lordships desire a simple reply, I will answer without distinctions. . . . Unless I am convinced by the testimony of Sacred Scripture or by evident reason—since I do not accept the authority of popes and councils, for it is evident that they have contradicted each other—my conscience is captive to the Word of God. I cannot and I will not recant anything, for to go against my conscience is neither right nor safe. Here I stand, I can do no other. God help me. Amen."*

The hall erupted with noise and confusion from both Luther's supporters and his antagonists. The angry emperor rose and the session ended. Luther returned to his lodgings and among his friends threw up his arms and exclaimed, "I'm through. I'm through." While the stand of Luther at Worms was a pivotal moment, the conflict was not over.

Luther would not see Charles again. His protest had travelled to the highest levels in the church and now to the highest levels of government. He had incurred opposition in both spheres. The next day, Charles responded by stating his own position written by himself and in French, "You know that I am born of the most Christian emperors of the noble German nation, of the Catholic kings of Spain, the archdukes of Austria, the dukes of Burgundy, who were all to the death true sons of the Roman Church, defenders of the Catholic faith, of the sacred customs, decrees and uses of its worship, who have bequeathed all this to me as my heritage, and according to whose example I have hitherto lived. Thus I am determined to hold fast by all which has happened since the Council of Constance. For it is certain that a single

*This famous speech is quoted in many places and some have claimed it to be the greatest moment in modern history. The wording will be slightly different in each citation, but all agree with the essential meaning and intent of Luther.

monk must err if he stands against the opinion of all Christendom. Otherwise Christendom itself would have erred for more than a thousand years. Therefore I am determined to set my kingdoms and dominions, my friends, my body, my blood, my life, my soul upon it. For it were great shame to us and to you, you members of the noble German nation, if in our time, through our negligence we were to let even the appearance of heresy and denigration of true religion enter the hearts of men. You all heard Luther's speech here yesterday, and now I say to you that I regret that I have delayed so long to proceed against him. I will not hear him again: he has his safe-conduct. But from now on I regard him as a notorious heretic, and hope that you all, as good Christians, will not be wanting in your duty" (Brandi 131-2).

No one among the supporters of Rome considered that Luther might have been right. All effort was focused on forcing Luther to recant. In the days that followed, a series of private conferences with many officials sought some reconciliation with Luther. Finally, with no breakthrough or change, Luther asked for and received permission to depart. On April 26 he left Worms for the return trip to Wittenberg.

Charles asked Aleander to compose an edict against Luther. It was held back until Frederick and a large number of other members of the Diet also left Worms. The edict was hurried through with the remaining members of the Diet who were loyal to Rome. It was drafted early in May and stated among other things that no one was to take Luther into their homes, receive him at court, offer him food, drink, help, support, or encouragement. Citizens of the empire were directed to seize him and send him to the emperor under strict security. The Diet adjourned on May 26, when Charles published the edict.

Charles next turned his attention to the threat posed by the invasion in the Netherlands. War began. It became a life and death struggle between two powerful European monarchs—Charles and Francis—and it would occupy the attention of Charles until he was finally crowned emperor by the pope in Bologna. ❦

1520

May 4, 1521

Luther, abducted and taken to Wartburg Castle, lives disguised as Knight George.

Dec 1521

Luther secretly visits Wittenberg.

Feb 1522

Luther's work *On Monastic Vows* published.

Dec 1521–Mar 1522

Luther translates New Testament into German.

Sep 8, 1522

Magellan's expedition returns to Spain.

Dec 1522

Rhodes surrenders to Suleiman the Magnificent.

1525

CHAPTER NINE

WARTBURG CASTLE

MAY 4, 1521—MARCH 3, 1522

hen the negotiations collapsed and it was clear that Luther's case had run into the stone wall of the emperor's opposition, Luther headed home to Wittenberg. The safe-conduct would expire on May 6. Charles had agreed to honor it, but Luther would soon be a fugitive from imperial power. The Edict of Worms identified Luther as a "reviver of the old and condemned heresies and inventor of new ones." He was accused of high treason and subject to severe penalties: the loss of property, arrest, imprisonment, and, if the treatment of other heretics is a guide, death. Citizens of the empire were directed to capture him and return him to the jurisdiction of Charles V. But the fierce will of Charles and the pope was not to be.

The edict also declared that if anyone, whatever his social status, directly or indirectly opposed the decree, he would also be guilty of high treason and subject to the same punishments. In spite of all its bluster, Frederick the Wise considered the edict illegal. The Emperor did not follow imperial procedures, and the edict was passed after Luther's supporters left Worms. Therefore it was not a united decision as it claimed to be.

Frederick had earlier developed a plan to hide Luther away temporarily. Spalatin shared the plans with Luther and counseled the utmost secrecy. Luther knew what was about to happen even if he did not know the details. On the morning of April 28, in a letter to Lucas Cranach written from Frankfurt on the way home, Luther asked the artist to thank the city council for the transportation they had provided. He also wrote, "I shall submit to being 'imprisoned' and hidden away, though as yet I do not know where" (AE 48, 201). Frederick also did not know where Luther would be kept so that he could honestly plead ignorance at court.

From Frankfurt, Luther's journey back to Wittenberg continued. Luther's party stopped in Eisenach, where Luther spent some time with his family and then resumed the journey. On May 4, horseman suddenly emerged from the forest and roughly took Luther. After taking care to conceal their escape route, they brought Luther to the Wartburg Castle and put him in a cell reserved for criminals under the watchful eye of Hans von Berlepsch, the caretaker of the castle. He was to be hidden there for his own protection. Since secrecy was essential, Luther was disguised as a knight. He was kept away from others until he had grown a beard and learned the ways of a knight. Then he became Junker Jorge to everyone.

Yet the need for secrecy remained. On occasion he signed his letters in Greek, and once he signed a letter to Spalatin as Henry Nescius (AE 48, 256). He did not always know where Spalatin was and did not want to risk having his letters intercepted by others. Later, when some believed they had discovered his whereabouts, Luther wrote a letter with false information in order to fool his enemies. The letter was then to be cleverly planted where his opponents could find it.

But Luther was safe, thanks to Frederick's ruse and protection. While at the castle, he anguished over not being in the fray. He did not relish being "in my wilderness . . . in the land of the birds" or "at his Patmos," as he sometimes referred to his exile. In the early months he suffered severely from constipation and received medicine for relief. The location of his wilderness may have been secret, but soon there would be no doubt that Luther was not dead but very much alive. He kept busy. He wrote and sent his work to the publishers in Wittenberg through Spalatin, his important contact on the outside. He also wrote letters to his colleagues in Wittenberg, especially Melanchthon.

Against Latomus

Since the Leipzig debate, the universities of Paris and Erfurt were assigned the task of deciding the winner. Erfurt, Luther's alma mater, refused. Paris took its time. In the meantime, the universities of Louvain and Cologne entered the arena with their own condemnations of Luther. Then, just before Luther appeared at the Diet of Worms, almost two years after the debate, the Sorbonne of Paris published its condemnation of Luther on April 15, 1521. They cited 104 errors in Luther's writings, which included works that appeared after the debate. The verdict of the university did not even mention the Leipzig debate and did not discuss the main issue of the debate: papal infallibility and authority. Duke George, John Eck, and the Roman Church were not pleased with the omission, but they rejoiced at the condemnation of Luther.

Melanchthon responded to the Paris decision with a powerful refutation and defense of Luther in Latin. The Sorbonne retaliated with disdain for the young boy of Wittenberg. They characterized him as a young man of 24, married, and small in stature. Their response also asserted that the University of Paris was the chief guide in matters of scriptural interpretation, because the Scriptures and the church fathers were obscure. Luther translated Melanchthon's response and the decision of Paris into German, adding his notes while at the Wartburg, and then sent it off to the printer. Luther was most certainly not dead.

Neither was the opposition to Luther. A member of the Louvain faculty known as Latomus wrote a book against Luther. It reached Luther shortly after he arrived at the castle. His criticism of Luther came from a scholastic scholar like Cajetan, but Latomus, whose real name was Jacobus Masson, cited Scripture passages to support his points, which Cajetan never did. Luther chose to respond in a writing simply titled *Against Latomus* (AE 32, 137-260). Without a library and his books, Luther could not check the quotations of Latomus or quote passages from church fathers except from memory. Luther wrote, "I have only the Bible with me" (259). Luther challenged the scholastic presuppositions and the distortions of the biblical text his opponent used to support his thinking. But Latomus had provoked Luther to think through the biblical concepts he had begun to express since his first protest. What he wrote was a clear, early expression of justification by faith.

Luther was convinced that Latomus and the sophists did not understand sin or the depth of the corruption within the human heart. Latomus and other Roman Catholic sophists believed that humans could perform what the commandments demanded. They claimed that after Baptism no sin remained, but only weaknesses that could be removed by the human effort of good works prescribed by the church, and those works would earn God's grace. He identified their teaching when he wrote, "They teach that so much can be effected by works actually performed, providing they are done with all of one's natural powers, that God necessarily and infallibly grants grace to them" (153-4).

Luther had begun to see things differently. Since his experience in the thunderstorm on the way to Erfurt, Luther had done all he could to earn the favor of God. Yet he was still deeply troubled by his imperfections. When he asked for help from his superior, John Staupitz encouraged him to turn to

Christ. Since that time, Luther's reading and study had convinced him to cling only to Christ. Latomus and the others were turning away from Christ and concentrating on their ability to keep God's commands. Luther objected. The result of their theology for Luther was that they claimed that " 'the commandments are completely satisfied so that forgiveness is not needed.' It is this which Augustine, and I, and the Scriptures deny" (157).

Luther, Augustine, and Scripture defined sin as a pervasive fault deserving God's judgment. Even the good works done by Christians are not perfect but polluted by sin. "Our good works are of such sort that they cannot bear the judgment of God" (172). Luther turned to Isaiah to defend his stance: "All our righteous acts are like filthy rags; we all shrivel up like a leaf, and like the wind our sins sweep us away" (64:6). He also turned to Paul's letter to the Romans for proof. Paul maintained that he was a sinner after Baptism in Romans 7:18: "I know that good itself does not dwell in me, that is, in my sinful nature." Luther wrote, that sin "is an evil guest, and yet it dwells within us, in our flesh, in our land, within our borders. Therefore there is nothing good in the flesh, indeed, as I said, there is nothing good, not simply a penalty, but sin" (249).

The commandments demand perfect obedience. No one can comply. All humans must despair of their own efforts. The commandments announce the harsh judgment of God on all disobedience whether done by believer or unbeliever and whether it was done before or after Baptism. By the harsh judgment on sin that the law announces, God "wants to drive and force all men to Christ so that they—trembling, desperate, and sighing—will shelter themselves under his wings. . . . All the saints tremble before this judgment. They perish unless they have Christ for a hiding place" (240). Only in Christ is there an answer to the dread sinners feel when faced with a holy, powerful, and righteous God.

Believers find full forgiveness in Christ, yet they continue to sin. So for the Christian, two forces oppose each other. Christians are always in battle array against this sin within, but they have the grace of God in Christ and cling to Christ for forgiveness. "Sin and trust [in God] are simultaneously present in us and in all our works as long as we are on this earth" (233). The Christian is saint and sinner at the same time. Believers cling to Christ alone, struggling against the sinful nature, and seeking to do what pleases Christ rather than the sinful nature. Christians do not trust in the works demanded by the human traditions of the church to obtain peace with God; that peace is a gift of God freely given in Christ.

In this struggle, the reigning principle in the life of a Christian believer is Christ and his forgiveness. The sin that clings to human flesh works against the forgiveness believers have by faith, and that sin "is a rebel and irksome to the ruling spirit" (251) or the new life Christians have in Christ. Yet this sin, deserving God's wrath, does not reign supreme within the believer. "No one's faith endures unless he relies upon Christ's own righteousness, and is preserved by his protection" (239).

Luther confessed that Christ is the answer to the sin before Baptism and after Baptism. The apostle Paul also says, "There is now no condemnation for those who are in Christ Jesus." (Romans 8:1). Luther maintained this is true, but not because of any human works that counterbalance human sin, such as the penance proscribed by a priest. No, sin is sin—always sin and always deserving God's judgment. But believers are not condemned, because Christ by grace forgives all sins—even those committed after Baptism. Sin is not imputed to the Christian. Instead, Christ's work covers it. In Christ, God has justified the sinner. "Even after forgiveness there is still sin, but it is not imputed" (209).

One can see the reason Latomus and others reacted so negatively to Luther. Not only did Luther oppose the power of the Roman hierarchy as he did at Augsburg before Cajetan, at Leipzig before Eck, and at Worms before the emperor, but he also pulled the rug out from under the everyday practices of the priesthood. Penance, confession, and the Mass were works that helped undo the weaknesses within. But they all were swept away by Luther's insistence on Christ alone. What that meant for the church and for believers, Luther would continue to clarify from the writing he did at his castle desk at the Wartburg and later in Wittenberg. He would certainly keep the printers in Wittenberg busy.

The Sermons, Melanchthon's *Loci,* and *On Confession*

Luther asked for and eventually received the books and papers he needed. His work continued. It just had to be done in exile. Many who embraced his protest and the reforms he advocated were still tied to the teachings and practices of Rome. They did not fully grasp the extent of Luther's emphasis on justification by grace. The people in the churches were hearing sermons that often had little to do with the gospel. That troubled Luther. Because he was a pastor at heart, he was concerned what everyday people were hearing in their churches. He desired to make sure that the preaching of the gospel took center stage. He knew that where the gospel was proclaimed, Christ and his power were at work to create, nourish, and empower faith. So he turned his attention to writing sermons for the Sundays and festivals of the church year. He sent his work to the printers in Wittenberg. The task of providing gospel centered sermons for parishes continued. Luther produced sermons long past his confinement at the Wartburg. Others who adopted Luther's focus on Christ and the Scriptures then used these sermons. They were widely used and counteracted false teaching and the poor training of the early parish preachers. They helped spread the seeds Luther had struggled to acquire and plant them in the minds and hearts of others.

One significant work by Melanchthon helped to water the seeds of Luther's ideas and then helped them to grow. His *Loci Communes,* or *Commonplaces,* was the first systematic exposition of the Wittenberg theology. It grew out of Melanchthon's lectures on Romans and clearly and thoroughly proclaimed sin, grace, repentance, and salvation. It was not a theoretical treatment of these topics with endless distinctions, definitions, and digressions, similar to Thomas Aquinas and the scholastic theologians. Instead, it was a practical approach based on the Scriptures. The first edition, published in 1521, did not deal with every theological topic. It did, however, become the standard text for theological students at Wittenberg and elsewhere among Lutherans. Subsequent editions expanded on the topics discussed. One of them, the edition of 1535, was even dedicated to Henry VIII to encourage the Lutherans in England (Schaff 7, 370).

Luther thought very highly of Melanchthon's work. He considered it "an unanswerable little book which in my judgment deserves not only to be immortalized but even canonized" (AE 33, 16). It is difficult to overestimate the importance not only of this work of Melanchthon but all his other works. He was a key figure in the growth of the Reformation.

On Monastic Vows and the Mass

Luther had already called into question the celibacy of the priests in *To the Christian Nobility.* Because of Luther's comments, a few priests had already chosen to marry rather than remain celibate. But they experienced opposition and persecution, even legal action and removal from office. On the authority of a clear biblical passage, Luther offered an answer to the question of whether priests should be forbidden to marry. Having 1 Timothy 4:1-3 in mind, he wrote to Melanchthon, "Paul speaks very openly concerning the priests. He says demons have forbidden them to marry. Since the voice of Paul is the voice of the Divine Majesty, I do not doubt that it must be trusted in this matter" (AE 48, 277).

The question of the celibacy of the monks was not so clear. Monks made a vow before God when they willingly agreed to remain unmarried. Priests had made no such vow, but were simply required to remain celibate. So Luther was not so sure that the same principle could be applied to monks who made a vow of celibacy. He searched the Scriptures for direction and an answer. "We are looking for a word of Scripture and a testimony of the divine will" (AE 48, 279). Luther's colleague in Wittenberg, Carlstadt, had written condemning the celibacy of the monks. But Luther was not convinced that his arguments were strong enough. He agreed in principle with Carlstadt but questioned his use of Scripture. After some inner struggles and letters back and forth on the subject with Melanchthon, Luther concluded that monks who had taken vows to gain salvation or righteousness by their vow were acting contrary to the gospel and God's will. Monks who took vows for such reasons could annul them. They could, of course, remain celibate if they wished to serve God without family obligations. Luther's colleagues in Wittenberg recognized at once what this meant: monks would suddenly become free to leave the monastery. And they did.

To explain his thought more clearly, Luther wrote the book *On Monastic Vows* near the end of 1521 and dedicated it to his father, Hans. Sixteen years earlier Luther had taken the vow to remain unmarried against his father's will and without his knowledge. His father was angry and chided his son because he had failed to keep another of God's commands: to obey his parents. Hans wondered if the vow Martin had taken to become a monk was because of an illusion or deception his son had followed. Now, 16 years later, Luther admitted that his vow was wrong when he wrote to his father, "Indeed, it was a wicked vow, and proved that it was not of God not only because it was a sin against your authority, but because it was not absolutely free and voluntary. In short, it was taken in accordance with the doctrines of men" (AE 48, 332). Luther's argument for other monks applied to himself and brought reconciliation with his father. But Luther remained celibate. To his colleagues in Wittenberg he joked that they would never give him a wife, and he chose to live as he was, at least for the time being.

During the exile in the Wartburg, Luther also turned his attention to the Mass as celebrated by priests. In Roman Catholic practice the celebration of the Mass was a sacrifice. In his *Babylonian Captivity of the Church,* Luther had already protested the abuses of the Mass, including its use as a sacrifice for sin offered by the priest. Part of the objection was that faithful Catholics paid priests to say Mass for their loved ones in purgatory or for the faithful still living. They maintained that the priest offered this unbloody sacrifice in order to minimize the satisfaction required for sin. These private Masses were to shorten the time a soul was to spend in purgatory. In a letter from the Wartburg he said that he would never celebrate Mass in private again. For Luther, the purpose of the sacrament shifted from a work earning release from punishment back to what the apostolic church originally taught. Scripture also taught that Jesus instituted the Lord's Supper as a gift offering full and complete forgiveness based on what he did. As Jesus said, he gave his body and shed his blood for the forgiveness of sins. The words recorded in the gospels and the apostle Paul's letters were the authority for the shift.

Luther raised an additional objection to the Mass as it was celebrated in Catholic parishes. The Roman Catholic Church decreed that the common people should receive only the bread, that is, in one kind. The priests received and drank the wine. Luther maintained what the Bible taught. People should receive the Sacrament as the Lord instituted it—in two kinds, bread and wine. The change to both kinds would come slowly. As the reformers were soon to discover, a sudden change would lead to confusion and turmoil.

Trouble in Wittenberg

All was well in the Wartburg, but all was not smooth in Wittenberg. In Luther's absence, Carlstadt proclaimed that receiving the Sacrament in only one kind was a sin. In December 1521 he caused a great deal of unrest when he celebrated the Sacrament in both kinds. For Wittenbergers it was a rash change that they did not understand. Carlstadt was anxious to return to the original Sacrament as quickly as possible, even if the people were not ready for the change. Unrest grew.

The trouble expanded beyond the Lord's Supper. Carlstadt also maintained that all religious objects were sinful. Riots broke out and many religious objects were destroyed. Students disrupted Mass and drove the priests from the altar. Discord threatened the public peace. Rebellion and disunity plagued Wittenberg. Luther wrote against it from the Wartburg, but the difficulties did not disappear. He expressed his pastoral concern and warned that rebellion and force would not bring about any reformation. New troubles also arose with the appearance of men from Zwickau who claimed they did not need the Bible because the Holy Spirit had spoken to them directly. Without Luther's leadership, the faculty of the university was unable to still the unrest and restore order and unity.

As the days progressed, it became clear that Luther had to return to Wittenberg even if it meant leaving the protection of Frederick and the safety of the hilltop castle. Luther informed Frederick that he would return to Wittenberg, but the elector wrote to Luther asking him not to return at this time. Luther was an imperial fugitive because of the Edict of Worms and had been excommunicated by the church. Yet Luther felt it was essential that he return to Wittenberg to help calm the unrest and restore order. He wrote to Frederick announcing his firm resolve to leave the safety of Wartburg for the unknown danger of Wittenberg: "I have written this so Your Electoral Grace might know that I am going to Wittenberg under a far higher protection than the Elector's. . . . Inasmuch as I do not intend to obey Your Electoral Grace, Your Electoral Grace is excused before God if I am captured or put to death" (AE 48, 391-2). He urged the elector not to resist the imperial authorities but do his duty as a Christian to obey those the Lord had established for the good of society.

While all this was going on, Luther had also begun to translate the New Testament. When Luther was ready to leave, he had finished the first draft of the New Testament. At the end of February he sent a portion of his translation—perhaps Matthew—back to Wittenberg and Melanchthon and prepared to return home. On March 1 he began the journey back to Wittenberg. ❦

1520

AUG 29, 1521

Belgrade falls to Turks.

MAR 1522

Luther returns to Wittenberg to restore order.

MAR 9, 1522

Luther begins Invocavit Sermons to calm Wittenberg.

SEP 21, 1522

New Testament printed.

JUL 1, 1523

Henry Voes and Johann Esch, first Lutheran martyrs, executed in Brussels.

1525

CHAPTER TEN

WITTENBERG, GERMANY

SEPTEMBER 21, 1522

uther left the Wartburg in the company of a couple of knights and dressed himself as a knight, wearing a red cap and breeches. He certainly did not look like a monk. They stopped at the Black Bear, a tavern just outside Jena. Luther mingled with the patrons, including two Swiss students. They did not recognize Luther, although they were curious. Luther sat at one of the tables, his right hand resting on the hilt of his sword, while reading from an open book before him. The book Luther read was a copy of the Hebrew Psalms—a curious book for a knight to read. The Swiss students wondered about this knight, but Luther kept up the ruse. They suspected this knight was not who he appeared to be. They admitted to the knight that they were on their way to Wittenberg and hoped to see Luther there. The Reformer suggested that they would indeed see Luther in Wittenberg.

When Luther finally arrived at Wittenberg, the elector sent Jerome Schurf, the court councilor, to meet with Luther and draft another letter to the elector that could be shared with the imperial government. This letter's intent was to clarify that Luther had returned without the elector's permission; Frederick did not want to be seen as giving Luther explicit permission to return as a fugitive. This letter, with its legal and imperial language, would allow the elector to retain his integrity and honor and still retain the Catholic faith he continued to confess. Luther complied, and the letter, it seems, was sent to Frederick's delegation to the imperial government.

The Swiss students also reached Wittenberg and quickly recognized the knight they had met at the tavern. This time Luther was not dressed as a knight but in more typical dress. He was no longer in a tavern but in surroundings appropriate for a scholar and professor.

Restoring Peace and Order

Luther, of course, had returned to face an important issue—the Wittenberg disturbances. Three days after returning, Luther took to the pulpit to deliver a series of eight sermons, called the Invocavit Sermons; the first one was delivered on March 9, Invocavit Sunday. Each day Luther preached another sermon directing the people of Wittenberg to abandon force in making changes. He urged them to trust patiently the silent work of the gospel. He addressed the issues that were at the root of the disturbances: the Mass, the vows of monks, the marriage of priests, destruction of religious images, eating certain foods, and the Sacrament in two kinds.

Luther pledged, "I will preach [the Word], teach it, write it, but I will constrain no man by force, for faith must come freely without compulsion." He also urged the people to follow his example: "I opposed indulgences and all the papists, but never with force. I simply taught, preached, and wrote God's Word; otherwise I did nothing. And while I slept, or drank Wittenberg beer with my friends Philip and Amsdorf, the Word so greatly weakened the papacy that no prince or emperor ever inflicted such losses upon it. I did nothing; the Word did everything" (Lull 421).

Luther and the others desired to purge the church of the abuses that had arisen in the last 300 years, especially those that had distorted the gospel. But they were not to do this by force or violence. Instead, they were to change church practices and traditions cautiously so that those who had not yet understood the reasons for change would have time to understand. For the time being, Luther advised, "Therefore no new practices should be introduced, unless the gospel has first been thoroughly preached and understood" (Lull 434). Patience with the gospel and love for those who were still not yet convinced should mark these changes. "When the Word is given free course and is not bound to any external observance, it takes hold of one today and sinks into his heart, tomorrow it touches another, and so on. Thus quietly and soberly it does its work and no one will know how it all came about" (Lull 434).

Luther's sermons were a success. Peace and order were restored. Communion in one kind was restored except for special services for those who understood the Lord's institution and could receive the Sacrament in both kinds—bread and wine. After more instruction, more reforms in church practices were introduced. The celebration of the Mass as a sacrifice quietly disappeared. Private Masses quietly disappeared. Even the people did not request a private Mass said for themselves or their departed loved ones in purgatory. Yet the marriage of the priests remained, and the monks were not required to return to their celibate cloisters.

The Radical Reformers

While Luther was away, new voices proclaimed a different, more radical message. Nicholas Storch, a weaver from Zwickau, claimed that Gabriel had appeared to him and had given him a special revelation and mission. Two others joined him, claiming direct revelation from God and the gift of interpreting the Scriptures. They came to be known as the Zwickau prophets. Like the Old Testament prophets, they warned of future disaster on all who were unfaithful. They taught that infant Baptism was only a sham and encouraged people to receive true Baptism from them so that they could then enter the true church. The message they proclaimed brought confusion. While Luther was still at the Wartburg, they left the confusion they had created in Wittenberg and moved to spread their message elsewhere.

When Luther returned, so did the Zwickau prophets. Nicholas Hausmann, a friend of Luther who was pastor in Zwickau, had opposed them in Zwickau. Luther wrote to encourage Hausmann's stand against these prophets: "I hope you are strong in faith and are growing daily in the knowledge of Christ. The 'prophets' who came from your [town] are striving for peculiar things; they are pregnant with monstrosities I do not like. If these should be born, they will cause no small damage. Their spirit is extremely deceitful and specious. The Lord be with us. Amen" (AE 48, 401).

The "prophets" sought out Luther, but their interview with him did not convince Luther that they were anything but false prophets. The Zwickau prophets did not trust the Scriptures as the only source of truth. What they claimed to have from God was different from what God revealed in the Scriptures. After their interview with Luther, they left Wittenberg and took with them their fanatical teachings. Sadly, the idea of direct revelation from God has plagued the church from the very beginning. It reasserts itself again and again when people abandon the Scriptures. Then often they listen to "prophets" who proclaim new and different teachings. Luther maintained the principle of testing the spirits (1 John 4:1) and rejecting whatever was contrary to what God revealed in the Scriptures.

The September Testament

Luther wrote his friend John Lang on December 18, 1521, while he was still at the Wartburg, that he was translating the New Testament into German. His work had begun sometime in November or December. Luther understood the difficulty he would face in translating the New Testament, but he had the relative quiet of the castle and many hours to spend with little interruption to work on the project. Luther used the Greek text, avoiding the Latin Vulgate of Jerome except for reference. Most likely he used the Greek text that was published by Erasmus. It seems that he had that text when he was kidnapped after the Diet of Worms. At the end of February, just before he returned to Wittenberg, the first draft was finished. He sent a portion of his work ahead to Melanchthon and brought the remaining pages with him. This feat—translating the New Testament in such a short time—was nothing short of remarkable.

Luther and Melanchthon worked at revising the draft almost immediately. Melanchthon was a better Greek scholar than Luther, and together they polished the New Testament draft Luther had written in seclusion. They asked for the help of Spalatin. From him they sought help finding simple German words for the Greek words. The goal was to make the translation as easy for the common people as possible. Because of Spalatin's connections with the Saxon court, they also asked for help with references to coins and the jewels mentioned in Revelation.

Their revision was ready for the printer—Melchoir Lotther—in early May. In early June, Luther sent Spalatin the complete gospel of Matthew for the elector and his son John. No other copies were available. Even the printers were not allowed to take a single page home with them. The translators were fearful that competitors would pirate their work before the project was finished. Soon three presses were busy working simultaneously to complete the work.

In addition to the translation, Luther wrote prefaces for each book of the Bible. The general preface for the entire New Testament was not completed until the last minute. The important preface for the book of Romans interrupted the numbering of the pages and was inserted near the end of the process. On September 21, 1522, the project was completed, and four days later (September 25) Luther sent the first complete New Testament as a gift to Hans von Berlepsch, the guardian, or captain, of the Wartburg. Lucas Cranach was named as the publisher, but the name of the translator did not appear. Ten picture initials from Cranach's studio—some used more than once—mark the beginning of each book except for Philemon and 2 Peter. Twenty-one full-page illustrations were included for Revelation. Melanchthon had attempted to find a map to include, but no map could be found in time. Luther, as was his custom, received no royalty for the translation. It's not clear how many copies of the first edition were printed, but estimates range from 3,000 to 5,000 copies.

The copies were expensive for the day, although exactly how much people paid is difficult to determine. Nevertheless, the September Testament was a huge success. By sometime in November the copies were sold out. A new printing appeared in December, which incorporated over 500 corrections. That printing is often called the December Testament. Revisions and corrections became an ongoing effort. The task was never finished. Luther founded a Bible club with his colleagues in Wittenberg to work on the Old Testament. They met once a week and invited other scholars on occasion and often Jewish rabbis for help with the Hebrew. The Old Testament was not completed until 1534.

The September Testament and the later December Testament revision became a best seller. More than 200,000 copies found their way into the hands of eager readers. Some have guessed that distribution for all the editions was over 300,000 copies. The new German Bible was more than just the text of the Bible. It was a kind of self-study Bible, since it included introductions or prefaces to each book as well as notes and comments in the margins.

One might expect that Luther's Bible was not well received by his opponents. It was Lutheran; it was not Roman Catholic. Duke George banned the Bible in his territory. He commissioned Jerome Emser to create a list of false teachings in Luther's Bible. Emser's list claimed 1,400 errors, but there were actually only a few hundred and they were mostly deviations from the Vulgate. Later, Emser published his own translation that simply used much of Luther's Bible and removed the prefaces and notes that were so offensive to Catholic readers. Other "Roman Catholic" versions also appeared, but they leaned heavily on Luther's work. Luther mused that even the Catholics were reading his Bible, but they weren't giving him credit.

Germans treasured the Luther Bible. It had an enormous influence on the spread of the Reformation. With Luther's Bible, Germans had a readable translation of God's Word. They read it and memorized it. It gave Germans a masterpiece—not only a spiritual gem that spread the gospel but also a masterpiece of German literature. Luther's work also profoundly influenced the German language and is considered today as a profound contribution to the German language and culture.

NORTH SEA

1520

Apr 27, 1522
Charles V defeats Francis I at La Bicocca.

BALTIC SEA

1524–1525
Peasants' Revolt.

Jan 21, 1525
Anabaptist movement begins.

Wittenberg

London

Feb 24, 1525
Charles defeats Francis at Pavia (Francis taken prisoner).

ENGLISH CHANNEL

May 5, 1525
Frederick the Wise dies. Brother John the Steadfast becomes elector.

1525
William Tyndale publishes English New Testament.

Jan 14, 1526
Treaty of Madrid. Francis freed but disavows treaty after reaching France.

La Bicocca

Pavia

ADRIATIC SEA

Mar 10, 1526
Charles V marries Isabella of Portugal.

Jun 26, 1526
First Diet of Speyer convened and suspends Edict of Worms against Luther and followers.

Rome

1530

MEDITERRANEAN SEA

CHAPTER ELEVEN

SPEYER, GERMANY

AUGUST 27, 1526

uther is the tip of the spear in Reformation history. He stood before the Diet of Worms alone and opposed the established authorities of church and state. His voice resonated with many who sympathized with the need for reform. Others would follow his lead—Zwingli, Calvin, Cranmer, Knox, and others. In many ways the story of the Reformation is the story of Luther, but it is also the story of powerful forces and powerful people besides Luther.

One hundred years earlier another man dared oppose the Roman Church. Jan Hus also stood and confessed his faith, but he was imprisoned and burned at the stake. In order to obliterate his memory, his ashes were thrown into the Rhine. But he was not forgotten; Husites even came to visit Luther after the Leipzig debate. Of course, many things had changed since the Council of Constance condemned Jan Hus. Among them was the political world. Powerful people arose in Europe—Charles V, Francis I, Henry VIII—a triumvirate of powerful European rulers. Frederick the Wise, often viewed as a small prince in Germany, was important. He was an elector, an imperial official with years of experience in imperial politics, and by no means a simple, rough German. But others were also important. Suleiman the Magnificent, ruler and military leader of the Turks, influenced Reformation events. The Roman Church had become part of the new political climate. Leo X, Adrian VI, and Clement VII, three successive popes, add a significant dimension to the story, not just as religious leaders but also as political leaders. Later, Paul III, the pope who followed them, would earn his own place in the history of the Reformation.

For many years, the tension between these powerful people prevented direct and consistent opposition to Luther and aided the progress of the Reformation. While the Roman Church and the Roman emperor wanted to crush the Reformation, neither did. Other issues diverted their attention and energy until the war over religious unity broke out after Luther's death. The events that prevented quick action against the Lutheran heretics protected the fledgling Reformation until it could stand against powerful opposition of church and state. Then the pope and the emperor were focused clearly on opposing it and free from many of the distractions that prevented their joint action earlier.

One important idea kept forcing emperor, pope, and others to stand in opposition to Luther and the Reformation. It was more than a simple religious question. It was also political. At the time, imperial unity was tied to allegiance to one church—the Roman Church. Deviations from the Catholic faith were considered treasonous and rebellious. Jan Hus disturbed the union of the church and state. Charles V and the pope considered Martin Luther in the same way—a disturber of the peace and unity of church and state. Religious freedom was not a concept shared by all. Lutherans during this time struggled to gain legal status for their beliefs and, therefore, protection under the law. It slowly came, but in the process it involved bloodshed in the defense of their faith, which was at odds with the old traditional faith of Rome.

The Italian War, 1521–1526

The Diet of Worms ended with an edict that made Luther and all who agreed with him outlaws. But the edict was never enforced. Luther was hidden in the Wartburg Castle by his monarch, Frederick the Wise. Other factors also prevented the edict from being enforced. During the Diet, the French started war against the emperor. Francis I claimed he knew nothing of the attacks first directed against the Netherlands. Intercepted letters later indicated the opposite. Eventually the French also sent forces into Italy. At the time, Charles V was away from Spain and directed his attention to the challenge of Francis I. But the situation in Spain was also a concern. In his absence, revolts plagued Spain. When Charles returned later to Spain, the uprising had been suppressed for the most part. Nevertheless, Charles had the task of raising the necessary troops and money for a military campaign and negotiating treaties to ensure his success. The conflict with Francis that started at the end of the Diet of Worms would end up being a long and difficult conflict played out in large measure in Italy and, therefore, involving the popes who sought to advance their families and either protect or extend their territory.

Leo X and Henry VIII were drawn into the conflict against France. Henry joined Charles on an unsuccessful offensive into northern France. To the south in Italy, the pope's forces succeeded in capturing Milan, but during the conquest, Leo X died. Adrian of Utrecht, the former teacher of Charles V, became Pope Adrian VI. But for Adrian, the Italian struggle was not as important as a unified crusade against the Turks. Adrian advised peace in Europe in order to focus attention on this threat. Concerning the Reformation in Germany, Adrian advised the speedy enforcement of the Edict of Worms, but the conflict with Francis, the challenges in Spain, and the threat of the Turks made it impossible for Charles to enforce the edict.

A joint Spanish and papal imperial army defeated the French at La Bicocca on April 27, 1522. The loss caused French forces to withdraw across the Alps and leave Italy to the emperor. In July, Charles returned to Spain and would not leave until July 1529. Before leaving for Spain, he set up a regency council in the Holy Roman Empire that was to govern while he was away from Germany. The emperor-elect appointed his brother Ferdinand as his deputy. This council was composed of 22 members who were elected for limited terms. Among other things, the council considered a long list of complaints or grievances that the Germans had lodged against the Holy See. The list was not new; it had been under discussion long before Luther. But discussion was the most that came from the list.

In spite of his victory over Francis at La Bicocca, Charles did not have everything his own way. In 1524 the French king launched a new offensive and entered Milan. But French influence in Italy received a major setback when the imperial forces of Charles destroyed French forces at Pavia on February 24, 1525, and Francis was taken prisoner. Charles brought him to Spain where he remained until he signed the Peace of Madrid in January 1526.

In the West—Germany and the Turks

Since Charles was occupied with the French and Italy, he could not eradicate the Reformation as he pledged at Worms. The wars also drained his financial resources. Paying soldiers and financing campaigns required money, some of which he borrowed from the Fuggers in Germany. Gold also came from the Spanish exploration and conquests of the new world, but its flow was not steady or enough for the emperor's campaigns. In 1521 Cortez had conquered the Aztecs in Mexico. Charles appointed Cortez as governor of the new territory that was called "The New Spain of the Open Sea." Yet the lack of money would plague imperial forces in Europe almost constantly.

For Eastern Europe, the threat of the Turks was real. Suleiman the Magnificent took Belgrade (1521) and Rhodes (1522). Belgrade became an important Ottoman military base for future operations in Hungary. The threat of the Turks sent shock waves throughout the Holy Roman Empire. A response became necessary. Charles V remained in Spain, but his brother Ferdinand as his regent in the east had the task of facing the Turks. With the Turks and Luther occupying the attention of Europe, a diet convened in Nuremberg (1522) with Ferdinand representing Charles. One of its major objectives was to organize opposition to the Turkish threat. But the diet did little. It ordered public prayers and levied a tax but authorized no soldiers to oppose the Turks

On the issue of Luther, Pope Adrian, to the delight of George of Saxony and others, demanded that the Edict of Worms be carried out. Adrian was a simple, sincere man—a pious monk and different from Leo X. He understood that the abuses in the Roman Church needed to be corrected. He opposed Luther but confessed the role of the Roman Church in causing the trouble: "We know that for some time many abominations, abuses in ecclesiastical affairs, and violations of rights have taken place in the holy see; and that all things have been perverted into bad. From the head the corruption has passed to the limbs, from the Pope to the prelates: we have all departed; there is none that doeth good, no, not one" (Schaff 7, 393-4).

This frank admission paralyzed the Roman Catholics in Nuremberg and froze any action against Luther. It also gave courage to those who supported Luther and reform. In addition, concern over the violence that had erupted in Wittenberg while Luther was at the Wartburg had diminished. Luther's return restored peace and stability. For this and other reasons, the diet refused to execute the Edict of Worms and demanded that the pope and the emperor, within a year, call a free church council in Germany to decide the religious issues. They ordered Luther to be silent until the council could be held and authorized the preaching of the gospel according to the approved fathers of the Christian church. Luther was pleased with the compromise with one exception. He objected to keeping silent when his opponents were not silent. He believed that the gospel was at stake. He wrote Elector Frederick that it had always been his purpose "to write, teach, preach, do, and promote nothing else but that which serves, and is necessary and useful for, the strengthening of God's Word and honor, and also of the holy, true faith, of the love of one's neighbor, and consequently of the well-being of all of Christendom" (AE 49, 40).

But the lack of action at Nuremberg was not the end of the matter. Adrian died on September 14, 1523, and his successor was Clement VII. Rome rejoiced at the ascension of Clement, who turned again to the policies and approach of Leo X, his cousin. A new Diet at Nuremberg in 1524 resolved to execute the Edict of Worms "as far as possible." Clearly, the efforts to suppress the Reformation were not over. It was an ominous signal. The specter of armed intervention to suppress the Reformation also arose in Germany. Alliances of Catholics and Lutherans soon began to consolidate opposing faiths. The reformers in Wittenberg objected to the alliance of Lutherans, fearing that it would result in more conflict and would not help the cause of the Reformation.

Additional trouble in Germany and Hungary also diverted the attention of Charles from the Reformation and focused it on other threats. While Charles and Francis struggled for control of Italy, Germany erupted in two tragic and bloody struggles.

First the knights revolted, hoping to spread the Reformation by force but also hoping to gain some economic freedom. The shrinking role of the knights and their dwindling financial options led them to take drastic action. Some of the knights were among Luther's avid supporters in the early days. The knights of Franz von Sickingen had escorted Luther at Worms. Now, under von Sickingen's leadership, the knights decided to attack the Archbishop of Trier. The attack failed, and the rest of the sad tale saw von Sickingen, Ulrich von Hutton, another prominent supporter of the Reformation, and the other knights defeated. Pillage and plunder describe the actions on both sides.

The second struggle was even more devastating to Germany—the Peasants' Revolt. The life of a peasant was difficult. In some cases peasants were little more than slaves, and the economic conditions worsened for them. They looked to Luther as their champion. His concept of "the priesthood of all believers" put all on the same level before God. But it also fed political and economic aspirations for a better life and for relief from oppression. Equality before God translated so neatly into a desire for economic equality, or at least a better station in life than they had as poor peasants. At first a few violent clashes erupted in some sections of Germany. The peasant's shoe became a symbol for their protest. Thomas Munzter fanned the dissatisfaction and unrest by preaching violent defiance against authority.

The peasants presented their demands in 12 articles. They were consistent with Christianity, moderate, and reasonable. Luther urged the peasants to pursue their goals peacefully. His advice followed the principles he had spoken in Wittenberg when he returned to quell the riots and unrest there.

Peace. Nothing is gained by violence, he had preached. In his *Treatise on Good Works* already in 1520, Luther had written, "War can be likened to fishing with a golden net—you never catch as much as you risk losing" (AE 44, 94)—a quote he attributed to Caesar Augustus.

Unfortunately, in the summer of 1524 the protest of the peasants took a violent turn. Eventually much of Germany was plagued with rebellion. The peasants turned palaces, castles, convents, and libraries into rubble. Emboldened by their early successes, they descended into a war with the princes. Their rebellion and destruction turned Luther into their opponent instead of their champion. He issued a vicious attack of words on the peasants, urging the magistrates to restore order at all costs. His language was not calm and reasoned as he urged the princes to restore order by force of arms.

The princes went to war—a war of vengeance against the peasants. They needed little encouragement. Many peasants were taken prisoner, tortured, and executed. The victims exceeded 100,000 by some estimates. The peasants felt that Luther had betrayed them. Some called him "Doctor Liar." At first Luther sought peace and opposed violence and rebellion. His words calling for the princes to restore order hurt the cause of the Reformation. While the peasants' desire for economic and political relief was reasonable and justified, the violence was not. The bloody defeat of the peasants was a brutal and graphic lesson on the dead end that would come with violence and rebellion.

Clement VII, Francis I, and Renewed Imperial Conflict

When the imperial armies of Charles defeated and captured Francis I at Pavia on February 24, 1525, it appeared peace might prevail. Francis went to Spain as the prisoner of Charles. After almost a year, Francis finally signed the Treaty of Madrid (January 1526). The treaty required Francis to abandon all claims in Italy and the Netherlands. He agreed to surrender his two sons as hostages to Charles in Spain to ensure his compliance with the terms of peace. Francis was released, but as soon as he reached French soil, he declared the terms of the treaty null and void, claiming he signed it under duress.

Clement VII, who earlier supported the efforts of Charles, released Francis from his obligations under the Treaty of Madrid. Charles was, of course, angry. He viewed the refusal of Francis to live by his word a breach of honor and demanded the French king meet him for a personal duel. That never happened. Clement, on the other hand, was fearful of the power of Charles in Italian affairs. Now he joined Francis in the League of Cognac to preserve the liberty of Milan and Italy. The Italian War restarted. France, with the aid and blessing of the pope, once again resumed the conflict.

Diet of Speyer, 1526

In view of the new situation, Charles wanted to leave Spain to address the problems: the renewal of the Italian conflict, the "German heresy," and the threat of the Turks. But he could not. His Spanish subjects were not ready to see the emperor head for war without leaving an heir for Spain. On March 10, 1526, he married Isabella of Portugal. Yet the challenges to his realm could not wait and needed some kind of attention. Charles called for an imperial diet to be held in Speyer for the summer of 1526. In spite of his desire to attend, he could not. Ferdinand, his brother, presided.

When the Diet convened, one familiar supporter of Luther was absent. Frederick the Wise had died on May 5, 1525. His brother John succeeded him as the elector of Saxony. For many years Frederick and John had shared the responsibilities in Saxony. John was familiar with all the previous history and was ready to assume the role of elector. So together with other supporters of Luther as well as opponents of the Reformation, John arrived at Speyer for the Imperial Diet. It opened with an impressive procession of princes and envoys on June 25, 1526. The agenda was simple. Charles had brought the leaders together to enforce the Edict of Worms and to put down heresy and rebellion.

But the next two months created a different conclusion. The quarrel between Charles and the pope weakened Roman Catholic opposition to the Reformation. Clement had chosen to side with Francis against Charles. This alliance encouraged the Lutheran princes to confess their faith, stand more firmly against their opponents, and work toward a more "Lutheran" conclusion. They were joined by the imperial cities that had accepted the Reformation. On August 27 the Diet unanimously adopted a compromise approved by Ferdinand.

They concluded that a general or national council should be convened to settle the church question. Until the council could convene and settle the issue, the Diet decided that each state would be free to live and believe as "he would be ready to answer for, before God and His Imperial Majesty" (Brandi 246). In the original text, the agreement included "before God *above all,*" but it was later crossed out. In effect, this set aside the Edict of Worms and allowed each ruler to decide the religious question for his own territory. It was a victory for the Lutheran princes who gained legal status in the empire for the first time, and it established a law of religious liberty or freedom. Lutheran princes acted on this decision; Catholic princes and the emperor had no intention of granting religious liberty and looked for a time to undo the decisions of the first Diet of Speyer. Luther felt that the decision gave him a reprieve from the charge of heresy at least for a season.

Two days later, August 29, the Ottoman Turks gained a significant victory at Mohacs. The Hungarian forces under the leadership of King Louis II were soundly defeated. Almost the entire Hungarian army was destroyed. Louis fell from his horse and drowned while in flight from the defeat. There was no heir to assume leadership. Louis was married to Mary of Austria, the sister of Charles V. Ferdinand was married to Anne, the sister of Louis. The royal house of Habsburg was keenly touched by the defeat. For the Turks, the victory led to their presence in eastern Europe for centuries. It also underscored European fear of the Turks and the potential threat the Turks represented to the rest of Europe. ❦

NORTH SEA

BALTIC SEA

1520

Apr 1523
Nine nuns including Katherine von Bora escape to Wittenberg.

1524
First Lutheran hymnal published.

Sep 1524
Erasmus publishes *Concerning Free Will.*

Wittenberg

London

ENGLISH CHANNEL

May 15, 1525
Peasants' Revolt ends in defeat at Frankenhausen.

Jun 13, 1525
Luther marries Katherine von Bora.

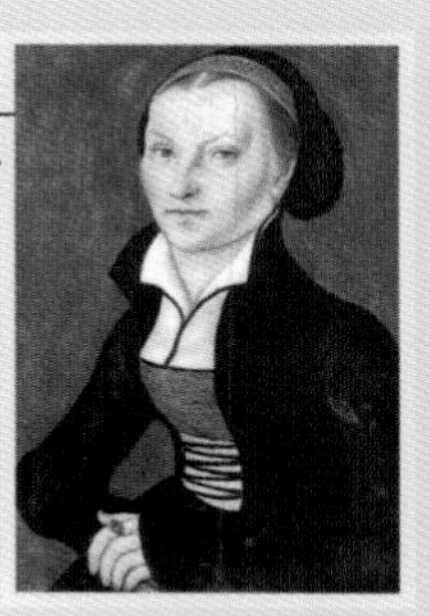

Dec 1525
Luther publishes *Bondage of the Will.*

Aug 29, 1526
Turks defeat Hungarian army at Battle of Mohacs.

ADRIATIC SEA

Jun 16, 1527
Instructions for visitation of churches prepared; printed Mar 22, 1528.

Rome

1530

MEDITERRANEAN SEA

CHAPTER TWELVE

WITTENBERG, GERMANY

JUNE 16, 1527

The political issues simmered in Germany and the empire. The first Diet of Speyer provided a compromise that received unanimous approval, but it was not to be a permanent compromise—a second diet would convene at Speyer. While political and military issues persisted, Luther confronted opposition to his teaching and sought to build an alternative church. He was not alone any longer. The princes had begun to assert themselves. Luther was not present at the first Speyer Diet, and he would not be at the second. His protest was no longer the voice of one man or even one faculty. It became a protest of many voices. Yet opposition from both the political and religious world continued to focus on those who protested.

Henry VIII

When Charles became emperor in 1520, he, Francis I, and Henry VIII had occupied center stage as kings apparently of one mind. Francis I soon put his military power in the field to oppose Charles V. The struggle with Francis was not religious but political. Francis remained Roman Catholic and so did France; Henry and England also were counted in the camp of Rome. Henry had been brought up Roman Catholic, and for now he was married to the aunt of Charles V, Catherine of Aragon. He put the Edict of Worms into effect in England and burned Luther's writings. Later, however, Henry played a different and important role in the Reformation history.

For now, Henry was Catholic. His opposition to Luther did not come as a political or military force. He wrote *Defense of the Seven Sacraments* (1521) in which he attacked Luther and his teachings. Luther recognized that Henry built his treatise on the same foundation as others who had opposed his teachings.

Henry cited the church fathers, church authority, and traditional scholastic scholarship without proof from the Scriptures. Unfortunately, Luther's attack was brutal and harsh and did more harm to Luther and the Reformation than to Henry. Luther's language was often an impediment to the cause of the Reformation and the gospel, and it still is. Without excusing his excesses, our generation of civility is sometimes one-sided in its criticism—looking with a blind eye to the side we favor. The age was given to excessively harsh language on all sides. We also judge earlier times on standards that are different from those at the time of the Reformation. Harsh language was still a problem 500 years ago, but today's standards eliminate almost all harsh and polemic language.

For the *Defense of the Seven Sacraments,* Henry was given the title "Defender of the Faith" by Leo X. Clement VII confirmed the title. But not unexpectedly, the title was revoked when Henry abandoned the Roman Catholic faith. His desertion from the traditional Roman Church altered English history and severed the ties to Rome and the papacy. The English Parliament reinstated the title. So today the king or queen of England still possesses the title. However, its meaning has changed. Leo intended it to mean "Defender of the Roman Catholic Faith." Today it means "Defender of the English Protestant or Anglican Faith."

Erasmus

Erasmus is a special case in the history of the Reformation. When Luther started translating the Bible in the Wartburg, he used the Greek text that Erasmus had published. Erasmus of Rotterdam was older than Luther and had already achieved a great reputation as a Christian humanist when Luther began his work as reformer. Like Luther, Erasmus protested the abuses of the Roman Catholic Church, but unlike Luther he felt he could live within the Roman Church as a critic. He tolerated Luther's harsh voice of protest, but his attitude cooled. For Erasmus, Luther was too obstinate and assertive. When Luther burned the papal bull in the bonfire of Wittenberg in 1520, Erasmus retreated from such bold action; he sought neutrality.

But he could not walk the middle road between Luther and the papacy for long. Erasmus was on friendly terms with the papacy and those in high places. They began to urge him to oppose Luther. Both Henry VIII and Duke George in Germany urged him to oppose Luther and his teachings. Erasmus responded by writing *A Discourse (Diatribe) Concerning Free Choice* in September of 1524. Luther was not anxious to respond. He had other responsibilities, and the impulse to respond was delayed until December of 1525 when he published *The Bondage of the Will* (AE 33, 15-295).

The difference between Luther and Erasmus expressed in these works is critical to understanding the gospel Luther proclaimed and the reason he was so sure of his position. Luther wrote in his response to Erasmus, "You have made me far more sure of my own position" (18). Erasmus wanted to accomplish two things. First, he wanted to maintain a position of neutral skepticism. Second, he believed that the human will by its own power was able to choose between good and evil; humans were able to make choices that would lead to eternal salvation. He quoted over 200 Bible passages that appeared to support his position, and he also claimed that the church fathers throughout history also taught the freedom of the will to make such choices.

But Luther's study of the Scriptures and the key understanding of justification by faith alone led him in the opposite direction. Luther complimented Erasmus for getting at the central issue. He wrote, "I praise and commend you highly . . . that unlike all the rest you alone have attacked the real issue, the essence of the matter in dispute. . . . You and you alone have seen the question on which everything hinges" (294). And the issue was whether God justifies the unworthy and sinful by his grace alone through Christ or whether God justifies humans because the sinner chooses to be saved by God. In his response, *The Bondage of the Will,* Luther replied to every passage cited by Erasmus and then provided his own passages to prove his position. Luther concluded that "free choice does many things, but these are nonetheless 'nothing' in the sight of God . . . in a man devoid of the Spirit there is nothing left that can turn toward the good, but only toward evil" (239, 293). Finally, Luther wanted to give God alone the glory for saving sinners. No human activity, not good works or even his pious choice, could claim to be a contributing factor. "To sum up: If we believe that Christ has redeemed men by his blood, we are bound to confess that the whole man was lost; otherwise, we should make Christ either superfluous or the redeemer of only the lowest part of man, which would be blasphemy or sacrilege" (293).

Luther also challenged the neutrality of Erasmus. Luther asserted clearly and thoroughly his position. Erasmus was tentative. Luther said simply, "It is not the mark of a Christian mind to take no delight in assertions; on the contrary, a man must delight in assertions or he will be no Christian. . . . Take away assertions and you take away Christianity" (19-21). Since both Luther and Erasmus cited Scripture, some might wonder if the Scriptures are clear and understandable without the interpretation of others. Erasmus said the Scriptures were confusing, but Luther explained that the message of Scripture is quite clear and "if the words are obscure in one place, yet they are plain in another; and it is one and the same theme, published quite openly to the whole world" (26). Luther demonstrated that the approach of Erasmus did not take advantage of the clear passages of Scripture.

Differences With Other Reformers

Henry and Erasmus represent the ongoing opposition the Reformation faced from those within the Roman Catholic Church. Once Luther stood boldly before Roman Catholic authorities in Worms, he opened the door for others to move away from Catholic teaching. The disturbances in Wittenberg while he was hidden away in the Wartburg Castle signaled a disturbing tendency among those who wanted to separate from Rome. Once free of Rome's discipline and threats, some also abandoned the standard of the Scriptures and developed their own teachings. The Zwickau prophets claimed special revelation and adopted teachings not found in the Scriptures. Thomas Muntzer had adopted some Reformation principles but used them to incite rebellion, disorder, and bloodshed.

Luther returned from the Wartburg and chastised the Wittenbergers for using force to spread Reformation doctrine. He remained opposed to the use of force to further the Reformation and asserted that the gospel must be preached: it alone would bring about God-pleasing changes. However, not all agreed with either his approach or his teachings. Carlstadt, a colleague of Luther's at the university, had instituted some radical changes in Luther's absence. Shortly after Luther's return, Carlstadt turned against Luther and began teaching that infant Baptism was wrong and that Christ's body and blood were not present in the Lord's Supper. He was not alone in these opinions but was joined by Ulrich Zwingli and John Calvin. Their views of the sacraments would remain and create division within the Reformation camp. The Sacramentarian Controversy, as it has been called, splintered the Reformation. Repeated attempts to bridge the differences would bring some together, but also would deepen the division for others. They would eventually take center stage at the Marburg Colloquy in October 1529.

Pigtails

The reforms in the church, almost from the beginning, included freeing monks and nuns from their vows. The monastery in Wittenberg became almost an empty building as monks left and were married or found other ways to support themselves. When Luther returned from his exile at the Wartburg, only one other monk remained in the Wittenberg cloister. The same thing happened all over Germany as the Reformation spread. According to both civil and church law, those who left the cloisters could be subject to the death penalty, but Luther continued to encourage monks to abandon the monasteries. The abandoned monasteries were put to use for other purposes. The Black Cloister, Luther's home as a monk, was given to Luther by the elector as his residence after his marriage.

When Luther freed monks from their vows, he had no plans himself to marry, but those plans changed. A group of nuns from a convent in Nimbschen began reading the Scriptures and came to treasure the gospel. At first they asked their parents for help in escaping the bondage of papal laws of obedience and celibacy. Three of them found family refuge, but nine found no safe haven. Yet they were determined and planned to escape. The convent was in the territory of Duke George, a fierce opponent of the Reformation, just across the border with Saxony.

The story of their escape has no doubt been embellished somewhat, but escape they did. Leonhard Koppe, a respected citizen, had a contract to deliver supplies, including numerous barrels of herring, from his home in Torgau to the cloister. He brought the loaded barrels to the cloister in a wagon and returned home with the empties. This routine became the opportunity for the nuns. The escape was well-planned, and the nuns became his cargo stowed in the empty barrels as he traveled across the border to Electoral Saxony. They arrived in Torgau on Easter Sunday and then went on to Wittenberg.

Luther accepted responsibility for their future. Marriage was one possibility for them, and Luther managed to find suitable husbands for some of them. One of them, Katherine von Bora, who was 24 years old already, became somewhat of a problem because she was independent and particular. For two years Luther proposed a number of possible suitors, but the matches Luther proposed did not prove successful. Luther had written to Spalatin from the Wartburg Castle in 1521, "They will never force a wife upon me" (AE 48, 290). In the middle of the Peasants' War and facing the threat of death at the hands of his opponents, Luther did not entertain any ideas of marriage. But suddenly he found himself "entangled in the pigtails of my girl" (Brecht, *Shaping* 199).

On June 13, 1525, Luther became legally engaged to Katherine in the Augustine monastery. It was Tuesday, the customary day of the week for a wedding. And weddings immediately followed the engagement. John Bugenhagen, who was present with a few of Luther's friends, performed the ceremony. Melanchthon was not present and at first was greatly distressed by Luther's decision. Reaction to his marriage by others was mixed. Some feared that he would destroy the progress the Reformation had made. His enemies, Duke George in particular, felt that the carnal pleasure of marriage was the entire reason for Luther's opposition to the papacy and its regulations. Later, Melanchthon changed his mind and accepted Katherine and the marriage.

Why did Luther take this dramatic step? He married to validate his teachings and, as he said, to spite the devil and the pope. He grew to treasure Katie and said he would not trade her for France or Venice. Luther also had his father's advice in mind. Hans Luther wanted grandchildren and was greatly distressed when his son abandoned the study of law to become a monk. But now Luther no longer sat alone in the Augustinian Cloister. Instead, he awoke to that pair of pigtails next to him. He would write years later, "I shall die as one who loves and lauds marriage" (Brecht, *Shaping* 200).

Luther's family grew like any other family. Katie gave birth to their first son, Hans, or John, on June 7, 1526. Luther's letters often refer to him as Hanschen (Little John or Dear John). Luther also announced that Katie had nausea during her second pregnancy. At the time, the plague ravaged Wittenberg. While many fled Wittenberg, Luther and his family remained. Katie gave birth to a daughter, Elizabeth, on December 10, 1527, but she lived only until the following August. Luther mourned her death with the deep emotion of a father: "My baby daughter, little Elizabeth, has passed away . . . so much has grief for her overcome me. Never before would I have believed that a father's heart could have such tender feelings for his child" (AE 49, 203).

In May of 1529, Luther announced the birth of his second daughter, Magdalen: "God, the Father of all grace, has graciously presented a baby daughter to me and my dear Katie" (AE 49, 218,219). Three more children would be added. Martin was born one day before his father's birthday on November 9, 1531. Paul arrived less than two years later on January 29, 1533, and finally, Margarethe was born on December 17, 1534.

Transforming the Church

During these years, the Reformation spread into new areas, but it also brought many changes and challenges. Some of these changes had occurred already in Wittenberg. The first was the quiet disappearance of Masses said in private. The papacy asserted that each Mass was an unbloody sacrifice for sin. In the process, the Mass was also purged of its sacrificial emphasis. Receiving both bread and wine was more difficult, however. For a time the people only received the Sacrament in one kind—the bread. After patient instruction, communicants received the Sacrament of the Altar in both kinds—bread and wine. Eventually, the practice of receiving both bread and wine became a hallmark of Reformation worship.

In contrast to worship in Roman Catholic territories, Luther also wanted the worshipers to actively participate in worship. In 1524 the first hymnals appeared. One was by a Nuremberg printer containing eight hymns, four of them Luther's. Another appeared in Wittenberg the same year containing 24 of Luther's hymns. Luther's desire, however, to move the liturgy from Latin to German was more difficult. He had already translated the New Testament into German, with the help especially of Melanchthon and Spalatin. The translation was a resounding success. Yet many people resisted changing the liturgy into their own language. At first the Latin liturgy was simply purged of errors but not changed to German. At Christmas in 1525 a German version of the liturgy appeared in Wittenberg. In February 1526 the elector mandated its introduction in parishes under his control.

The Reformation, which had started as a protest against indulgences, abolished them where the Reformation held sway. Eventually, the worship of saints, images, and relics disappeared. These, together with pilgrimages, private Masses, and Masses for the dead in purgatory, were abolished. Only two sacraments remained of the seven still found in Roman Catholic theology. The principle was to remove whatever could not be supported by the Scriptures but to retain practices and traditions that were helpful and beneficial to Christian faith. It was not a revolution but a reformation that sought to reestablish what was originally part of the New Testament church of the apostles and to keep what had developed over the centuries that was not contrary to the Scriptures.

But these improvements did not happen all at once. As the Reformation spread beyond Wittenberg, it became clear to Luther and others that the church had to be transformed in many additional ways. One of the most immediate challenges was that many pastors were poorly paid; the burden for their pay was no longer the sale of Masses and indulgences or the revenue from Roman Catholic lands.

Another was consistent and thorough teaching of Reformation truths. Luther was not in favor of legislation to correct the problems and to mandate solutions for the challenges. Instead he asked the elector to conduct a visitation of all the churches in Electoral Saxony in order to address the challenges of moving from the Roman Catholic teachings and practices to those of the Reformation. It was a logical request since the Diet of Speyer in 1526 had left the responsibility for reform to the rulers of the individual territories. What came out of these discussions with the elector and the other reformers was a set of instructions for visitors. It was prepared by June 16, 1527, but because of delays, including a shortage of paper, *The Instructions for the Visitors of Parish Pastors in Electoral Saxony* was not published until March 22, 1528.

This document was significant for the Reformation in Saxony and other territories. It created the discipline for pastors and parishes at a time when there was no consistent Reformation practice in the parishes. It was revised and improved from its first printing. As the visitations were carried out over the next few years, they revealed the unfortunate conditions in the parishes and schools, some of which were leftovers of Roman Catholic neglect, but they also set the agenda for solutions and improvement. The effort begun by these visitations shaped the future of the Reformation when it could have been swallowed up by determined Roman Catholic opposition. ❦

1525

May 6, 1527
Sack of Rome by unpaid imperial forces.

Jun 16, 1527
Instructions for church visitations prepared, with approval of Elector John of Saxony.

1529
Turks lay siege to Vienna.

1529
Luther's catechisms published.

Mar 15, 1529
Second Diet of Speyer convened.

Apr 20, 1529
Lutherans protest Diet's decision to reinstate the Edict of Worms.

Apr 25, 1529
Lutherans file official document of protest.

1530

CHAPTER THIRTEEN

SPEYER, GERMANY

APRIL 20, 1529

he first Diet of Speyer in 1526 provided a compromise that received unanimous approval. Roman Catholics and Lutherans were still in opposite corners. Catholics were not ready to concede the shelving of the Edict of Worms and allow the Lutheran heresy to continue to gain adherents. While Catholics consolidated their opposition, Lutherans also consolidated their position. As Lutherans understood the Diet's compromise, they began to strengthen the parishes through the visitations in Saxony. The divisions between the two were no longer lines in the sand; they were fortresses defended. During this time, it seems that many began to think that the next confrontation would be more than a battle of words and teaching.

While Germany began to sense the next confrontation between Lutherans and Roman Catholics, Charles was involved in another war with Francis over control of Italy. The League of Cognac pitted Francis and the pope against Charles. At first the renewed conflict with France, the pope, and the Turks kept Charles from devoting his full attention to the Reformation and enforcing the Edict of Worms. He was absent from the scene of the struggle. He remained in Spain during most of the conflict, but his forces achieved success, even if it was not complete success.

The Sack of Rome

This phase of the Italian fighting with France brought France and the pope together against Charles. The alliance between Francis I and Pope Clement VII was more than a personal blow to Charles V. He complained that he had wanted nothing but to support the papacy and establish one unified church. His efforts to oppose the Reformation could not be doubted.

His resolve during the first war with Francis and his ongoing struggle with the Turks in the Mediterranean had not wavered. Charles said he had no desire but to live and die as a good Catholic and did not wish to oppose an army fighting under the banner of the pope. The pope's turn toward Francis was political, not spiritual. The conclusion of the first war with Francis left Charles holding the power in Italy. Clement and the rest of Italy feared the power of the emperor and the loss of their own power. Clement's shift was nevertheless more than a little disappointing to Charles. He was indignant.

As much as Charles tried to point to the unfinished task he shared with Clement—the destruction of Luther and the Reformation—the pope and the allies of the League of Cognac pursued a course against him. Charles had forces in Italy to enforce his imperial rule after the first war, but those imperial soldiers were unpaid and starving. When the commander died, the army became a marauding band seeking food and plunder. No force was able to check their advance when they turned toward Rome. For these undisciplined troops, Rome was more than the seat of an enemy of the empire. It was also a prize and the source of food and money. On May 6, 1527, Rome fell.

The aftermath was devastating and appalling. The renegade and unchecked imperial forces plundered Rome. Thousands died. Rape and looting continued for many weeks during the rampage. The pope escaped to Castel Sant'Angelo but was kept in confinement until he escaped dressed as his chamberlain. He remained in exile at Orvieto and Viterbo for almost a year before returning to Rome.

Charles was embarrassed by the actions of his troops and forced to apologize. Luther wrote, "Rome and the pope have been terribly laid waste. Christ reigns in such a way that the emperor who persecutes Luther for the pope is forced to destroy the pope for Luther" (AE 49, 169). But he also wrote, "I do not want Rome to be burned" (AE 49, 176). Melanchthon grieved over the destruction. He did not blame the emperor but the army for the sack and concluded, "Whatever be the sins of the Pope, Rome should not be made to suffer" (Schaff 7, 689).

This event was a major factor in bringing the second war with Francis to an end. The political aspirations of the pope suffered a humiliating blow, and Francis was unable to pursue his goals in Italy. Yet the tragic events in Rome eventually gave success to the emperor. It eliminated the pope from the war and weakened the League of Cognac. In the end, both Charles and Francis were war weary and had depleted their resources to make war. The Peace of

Cambrai was signed on October 30, 1529. The treaty has been called the Ladies' Peace because Margaret of Austria, the Regent of the Netherlands, and the French Queen-Mother, Louise of Savoy, negotiated it. As he sensed the successful conclusion of the war, Charles left Spain for Italy with two things on his mind—the Lutheran heresy and the Turkish threat.

Pack Hoax

Perhaps in such a time of tension, it is not surprising that suspicion and fear would test everyone. Rumors of alliances between pro-Roman Catholic princes and counter alliances between pro-Lutheran princes were not uncommon. In fact, both sides were moving in the direction of such alliances. In 1528, Otto von Pack, an official of Duke George of Saxony, Luther's persistent opponent in Germany, became an embarrassing part of the tangled political situation.

For whatever reason, he turned over to Philip of Hesse, a supporter of Luther, a forged copy of a letter that revealed a threat against the Lutherans. It appeared to be signed almost a year earlier by pro-Roman Catholic princes in Breslau outlining a plan to oppose the Reformation by force of arms. Philip hurried to Elector John in Saxony with the document. They signed an alliance, mobilized for war, and planned a preemptive strike against the Catholic League. The Catholic princes who were to have signed the document denied having anything to do with it.

Before the trumpets of war sounded, Elector John of Saxony consulted Luther about the plan to go to war. Both Luther and Melanchthon opposed the military option and encouraged a wait-and-see policy together with diplomatic and legal efforts to bring peace instead of war. Luther wrote, "War does not gain much, but loses much and risks everything. Gentleness, however, loses nothing, risks little, and gains everything" (AE 49, 196). Peace prevailed. The hoax only raised suspicions and questions. A peace treaty was signed at a meeting in Smalcald in early summer 1528. Interestingly, reparations were paid to the Lutherans to cover the cost of their mobilization for war (AE 49, 198n).

Luther's Catechisms

From the beginning Luther did not want to establish a new church but to return the church of his day to its origins—the apostolic New Testament church—at least as far as its teachings were concerned. Yet as each day passed, it became more and more evident that the Roman Catholic Church was not willing to abandon the teachings and practices that had developed over the centuries. Indulgences, papal authority, and dependence on tradition, even when it contradicted the Scriptures, were examples. When the Roman Catholic Church insisted on the enforcement of the Edict of Worms, it was clear that reform of doctrine and practice was not a priority. Instead, like most organizations, the Roman Catholic Church was only interested in self-preservation and silencing criticism, not in reform. It simply followed the practice it had developed over the centuries.

Slowly the reform of the church took place in areas controlled by Luther's supporters. The visitations conducted in Saxony under the aegis of Elector John the Constant revealed the enormous task of reforming the parishes. The people were largely ignorant of Christian teaching, and many of the clergy, some of whom had only recently embraced the Reformation, were not grounded in the teachings of the Scriptures and the early church. Something had to be done. Melanchthon's *Loci* was an important presentation of God's truth for the university students, but the parish pastor and the common people needed a simple and practical resource for instruction. Even before the visitations, Luther had envisioned a simple handbook for the clergy and set to work on what came to be called the *Large Catechism*.

As he wrote, Luther preached a series of sermons on parts of the catechism and completed the Large Catechism in April of 1529. It was revised and eventually joined by the Small Catechism later that year. Both catechisms quickly became important tools to teach Christian truths and became handbooks for Christian living. The Small Catechism was directed at families and included daily prayers and a "Table of Duties." Luther added, "The head of the family should teach it in the simplest way to those in his household." The subjects touched on in the catechisms were common to the Christian tradition: the Ten Commandments, the Apostles' Creed, the Lord's Prayer, the sacraments, and absolution. Luther did not seek to supplant teachings that had long been accepted by Christians over the centuries. He sought instead to base them on what the Scriptures taught and purify them from Roman Catholic tradition and doctrine.

The Diet of Speyer 1529

While Charles was still wrestling with the Italian problems, he called for another diet at Speyer. It was to open on March 15, 1529. Two of the issues on the agenda were the Turks and the progress of the Lutheran heresy. The Lutheran princes were in the minority at the second Diet of Speyer, and the Roman Catholic princes wanted to reverse the policy of religious tolerance adopted in 1526.

Charles designated his brother Ferdinand to preside and sent instructions that were more open to the Lutheran princes. However, the instructions arrived too late for the opening of the Diet. The ship bearing the document was delayed for weeks by storms. In the absence of those instructions, Ferdinand adopted a much harsher position. Leaving the impression that he spoke in the emperor's name, he condemned the way the Lutheran princes used the compromise of 1526 and denied them the right to choose religious reforms. He ordered that no new reforms be allowed until a council could be called and reinstated the Edict of Worms. He also threatened total annihilation of the Anabaptists and followers of Zwingli. Ferdinand's goal was to suppress all dissension and create a united empire and united church in order to oppose the advance of the Turks, who would later lay siege to Vienna.

After weeks of discussion, on April 19 the majority accepted the proposal to revoke the Edict adopted at Speyer in 1526. Lutheran princes were told that they should yield to the fair and proper decisions of the majority. They, however, rose and left the hall. They objected. After a caucus they returned to voice their objection. Ferdinand forbade a full reading of it, and he and his commissioners left the hall. The Lutheran leaders nevertheless read their protest against the decision of the majority. The next day they presented the "Letter of Protestation," which Ferdinand also refused to accept or allow to be read. It was later printed and made public.

The Lutheran princes protested because the decision in 1526 was approved unanimously. They argued, "Such a unanimous vote cannot be and may not be altered with honor, reason and justice, except by unanimous consent." But the protest was more than a protest based on legal principle. It echoed the protest of Luther standing alone before the Diet of Worms in 1521.

They pledged obedience to the emperor in "all due and practical things" but "such things as concern the glory of God and the welfare and salvation of the souls of every one of us; as to these, by the command of God, for the sake of our consciences, we are in baptism and moreover in his holy divine word, pledged and bound to hold before all our Lord and God as highest King and Lord of lords." They clearly protested the Roman Catholic understanding of the Mass and asserted that the Sacrament they practiced was founded on Scripture and in accord with the institution of Christ. They pledged that "only the word of God and the holy Gospel of the Old and New Testaments, as contained in the biblical books, shall be preached clearly and purely, and nothing that is against it." They suggested that "a free ecumenical, Christian council, or at least a national assembly, should be held as soon as possible" to settle the differences (quotes are taken from the Northern Catholic Archives copy of English translation).

Six princes and 14 imperial free cities now shared Luther's protest. On April 24, the last day of the Diet, the decision of the Diet to reinstate the Edict of Worms was once more publicly read but without a mention of the protest. On April 25 the protestors drew up the official document of protest and had it notarized. As long as the appeal was pending, the decision of the Diet was unenforceable. They also sent the protest to Charles, but he did not listen and imprisoned those who delivered it. From this point forward, those who objected to the Roman Catholic Church and to the enforcement of its doctrines by the state were called Protestants.

The clouds of military opposition began to build and loom ominously on the horizon. One monk's protest was now shared by many others who had published their own official protest to an imperial diet. ❦

1520

OCT 11, 1520

Henry awarded Defender of the Faith from Leo X; opposed Luther at first but later made England Protestant.

OCT 1-4, 1529

Philip of Hesse hosts Marburg Colloquy.

JAN 30, 1530

Charles calls for diet at Augsburg.

FEB 22 AND 24, 1530

Charles V officially crowned emperor at Bologna by Clement VII.

MAR 7, 1530

Henry VIII's divorce request denied by pope.

APR 15, 1530

Lutheran delegation arrives in Coburg. Melanchthon, a collaborator with Luther, wrote the Augsburg Confession.

JUN 25, 1530

Augsburg Confession read before emperor.

1535

CHAPTER FOURTEEN

AUGSBURG, GERMANY

JUNE 25, 1530

The political power had shifted away from the Protestants. The Diet of Speyer of 1529 had reinstated the Edict of Worms, which accused not only Luther but also all who supported him of high treason *(lese majeste)*. The Catholic faction believed that Luther and his followers "wanted to raise factionalism, dissension, discord, crimes, wars, and evil things among Christians" (Edict of Worms). The punishment for such a crime included seizure of all goods and belongings "regardless of person, degree, or privilege." The edict also promised generous rewards for those who assisted in carrying out the imperial decree. The ominous specter of military action against the Reformation grew. The emerging victory of Charles in Italy contributed to fears that the Reformation might depend on the sword and not only on the Word.

The Edict of Worms, however, had been unenforceable since its adoption, with Charles in Spain and conducting military operations against Francis in Italy. The delay in implementing the edict allowed the Reformation to grow. Yet although the Diet of Speyer affirmed the edict in 1529, its hard line against Luther and his followers was still difficult to enforce without the force of arms. The hard line of the Catholics bred another hard line of the Protestants. Any effort to enforce the edict at this point carried with it the real threat of civil war in the empire.

The Marburg Colloquy

The German reformers, the Swiss reformers, and others across Europe had one common objective: reforming the abuses of the Roman Catholic Church and the papacy. But not all the reformers were theologically in complete agreement. Two different and significant camps emerged among the reformers. The issue was the definition of the Lord's Supper and the approach to the Scriptures. Zwingli, a Swiss reformer, and Luther in Germany were the primary protagonists. Zwingli's view of the Lord's Supper asserted that the body and blood of Jesus were symbolically represented by the bread and wine. Luther's view was different. He held to the words of Jesus in their plain and simple sense: "This is my body" and "This is my blood." Luther contended that those words do not allow for a symbolic interpretation. Because Jesus said that his body and blood are present in the Sacrament with the bread and wine, they are present just as he said. Even if Luther could not fully understand how, he held to the words of institution.

Sensing future military conflict with Roman Catholics, Philip of Hesse wanted to unite the two opposing views in order to provide a united front against the opposition of Charles and the Roman Catholics. In June of 1529, Philip invited scholars from both sides of the Protestant group to Marburg to work toward some agreement. Luther and Melanchthon were concerned that such a meeting would only deepen the division rather than bridge it. Nevertheless, the Wittenberg theologians and the supporters of Zwingli both accepted Philip's invitation.

Both parties arrived at Marburg at the end of September. The first discussions took place on October 1, and additional discussions stretched through October 5. Of course, the principal issue was the Lord's Supper. Early in the discussions, Luther wrote, *"Hoc est corpus meum"* (This is my body) in chalk on the table and covered it. For Luther, those words—the words spoken by Christ—were central. Since Scripture gives no indication that the words are to be taken symbolically, they must be taken literally. But for Zwingli and the others these words were not central. They turned to Jesus' words in John chapter 6 to prove a spiritual presence. But Luther and the others countered by saying that John chapter 6 does not refer to the Sacrament at all. For one thing, they were spoken before the Sacrament was even instituted. When Zwingli wanted scriptural proof from his opponents that Christ's body and blood are in the Sacrament, Luther uncovered what he had written on the table and exclaimed, "Here is our scriptural proof. You have not yet moved us" (Brecht, *Shaping* 331).

On October 4, near the end of the discussions, Luther sent a note to Katie in Wittenberg. "Dear Sir Katie! You should know that our amiable colloquy at Marburg has come to an end, and we are in agreement on almost all points, except that the opposition insists on affirming that there is only simple bread in the Lord's Supper, and on confessing that Jesus Christ is spiritually present there. Today the Landgrave [Philip] is negotiating [to see] if we could be united. . . . I am very busy, and the messenger is in a hurry. Say 'good night' to all, and pray for us! We are all still alert and healthy, and live like kings. Kiss Lenchen and Hanschen on my behalf" (AE 49, 236-8).

As Luther and Melanchthon feared, the discussion did not reach an agreement on the Lord's Supper. Philip considered unity against the Catholics important. His efforts at "negotiating" included a request that Luther draw up articles on which they might agree. Luther complied and drafted 15 articles on October 4, 1529. Both sides asked for forgiveness for words spoken harshly, and both sides admitted that they desired peace, but the disagreement on the Lord's Supper could not be resolved. Yet Luther's 15 articles, the Marburg Articles, revealed the depth of their agreement. Both sides agreed on 14 of the articles. But the difficulty posed by the last article on the Lord's Supper—whether the body and blood of Christ are really present in the Sacrament or only symbols—revealed their deep disagreement. Luther preached before leaving on October 5. He emphasized what the two sides had in common and avoided antagonizing those who disagreed. But there would be no united Protestant front against Charles and the Roman Catholics.

The Coronation of Charles in Bologna

While all the preparations for the colloquy were unfolding, Charles left Spain and made his way to Italy at the end of summer. The forces opposing him in Italy—including those of Pope Clement VII—no longer posed a threat, and Charles had emerged victorious. Peace had been restored. In May, the Turks with a large army had launched a campaign toward Vienna. But the siege of Vienna was unsuccessful. Suleiman's large army had encountered not only the valiant efforts to defend Vienna but also disease and bad weather. His forces limped back to the territory they had gained in Hungary. The news bolstered the emperor. When he arrived in Italy, the towns honored him enthusiastically on his way to Bologna, where he met with Clement.

Charles and Clement negotiated for four months from December to March. Understandably the negotiations were difficult. Charles still had a deep respect for the papacy, even though Clement participated in an alliance against him. Clement was in Bologna because imperial troops had ravaged Rome. Charles, along with many in Europe, believed that the Roman Church was in need of reform. Clement and the Roman curia were still unconvinced of the need for reform. The Protestant opposition to both Charles and Clement meant they needed to rebuild their alliance. They needed to succeed where the Protestants had failed at Marburg.

If Charles and Clement could reach an understanding, perhaps together they could address the nagging problem of the German and Swiss reformers. Charles believed the church was in need of reform, and most agreed with him. A church council that would address the grievances and remove the abuses still seemed to offer a way to unity for all. Charles renewed the proposal with Clement, but the curia and the pope remained cool to the idea. They had the reform councils of an earlier age in mind. Once such a council was convened, it could decide against them. Those earlier reform councils had deposed popes when there were two different popes at the same time—one in Avignon and one in Rome. If a council was necessary, Clement and the Roman curia wished it to be a council that was under their control.

From the reformers' perspective, they felt that since the papacy was a large part of the problem, a council under the aegis of Rome could achieve no real reforms unless it was free from papal control. Their hope was that at a true reform council all could participate without interference from the Roman curia and its head—the pope. Yet Luther, even in the very beginning, and other reformers later, proposed a council to heal western Christianity and bring both sides together.

On January 30, 1530, while still conducting the negotiations with Clement, Charles issued a summons for a diet at Augsburg. The diet was to "settle disputes . . . to hear, understand, and weigh the opinion of each man with love and charity, and thus come to live again in one Church and one State" (Brandi 306). The invitation reached Saxony and Elector John on March 11, 1530. The tone of the summons provided a sweet hope for the reformers after the sour disappointment of Speyer only a year earlier. Charles may have harbored the hope of avoiding conflict, but some of his supporters suggested that only force could bring about "one Church and one State." He may also have been extremely naive about the depth of the division in the church and its implication for the state. But church and state were his agenda. Unity was paramount in order to confront the other threat. The Turks were repulsed and driven from Europe, but not defeated. They persisted as a threat.

Finally, Clement crowned Charles, who had become emperor-elect in 1519, in Bologna as Holy Roman emperor. The coronation would normally have occurred in Rome, but Rome was still recovering from the sack by unpaid imperial soldiers in 1527. And since Charles was determined to call a diet in Augsburg, moving the coronation to Rome would have required additional time. The spectacle of the coronation was magnificent. The procession was depicted in frescos on the walls of churches and town halls all over Italy. Both emperor and pope appeared in the splendor of their ceremonial robes. On February 22, Charles received the iron crown of Lombardy from the pope; two days later, on his birthday, Charles was crowned Holy Roman emperor. Only a few German princes were present because the coronation was done quickly in order to allow the emperor time to head toward Germany. The Diet of Augsburg awaited him. It was not a council, but perhaps it could be viewed as a step in that direction.

All Travel to Augsburg

Political leaders from all over the empire made preparations to attend. Elector John of Saxony prepared to meet whatever lay ahead in Augsburg. Before he left, he wanted to formulate a statement that clearly expressed his faith and the faith of the Wittenberg reformers. He asked Luther, Melanchthon, Justus Jonas, and Johann Bugenhagen to present their thoughts at Torgau, the elector's residence. They drafted a preliminary document, called the Torgau Articles, before they left for the Diet. Earlier, in October 1529, the Wittenberg theologians drafted another statement of beliefs called the Schwabach Articles. They were 17 articles of faith prepared for a meeting to seek a defensive confederation to oppose potential Roman Catholic and imperial forces. At that point Luther and Melanchthon opposed any military action, fearing it would only escalate the conflict. The Schwabach Articles and the Torgau Articles, together with the Marburg Articles, helped inform the delegation that hoped to confess their beliefs in Augsburg.

Luther and his colleagues made their way toward Augsburg and arrived at Coburg on Good Friday, April 15. Coburg was still in Saxon territory, under the control of Elector John, and close to Augsburg. Elector John sought to get even closer and asked if the Saxon delegation, with Luther, could stay in Nuremberg, a free imperial city about 100 miles closer to Augsburg. But the city chose not to host the delegation. It pledged not to abandon the Reformation teachings, but simply did not wish to create additional trouble with the emperor. Because Luther was still an outlaw, he could go no closer and still remain under the protection of the elector. Elector John reasoned that even at Coburg, 150 miles away from Augsburg, Luther was close enough to communicate with the delegation.

While Luther remained at the Coburg Castle with Veit Dietrich, his secretary, the others turned their attention to the Diet and traveled to meet whatever awaited them. The Lutherans were armed with the documents they hoped to use in crafting a confession once they arrived at the Diet. Melanchthon headed the theologians from Wittenberg, and together with

John the Steadfast, the elector of Saxony, and other political leaders, they arrived in Augsburg on May 2, apparently the first delegation to arrive. Charles, however, was delayed.

Before the Diet convened, the Lutherans had learned that the pope was attempting to derail any serious discussion of the religious issues. He only wanted the "heretics" condemned. In addition, John Eck, who had earlier opposed Luther at a debate in Leipzig, wrote a lengthy attack against Luther and those who stood with him. His *404 Articles* attempted to paint the reformers as the worst of heretics and treasonous rebels. He and others viewed the Reformation as a threat to the empire. Eck's attack convinced Melanchthon and the others to present a gentle and positive response instead of an angry denial of the charges leveled against them by Eck and others.

When Charles V approached Augsburg, a large delegation, including the Lutheran princes, greeted him outside the city. The pope's ambassador unfurled the papal banners to offer a blessing from the pope. Charles and the others knelt. The Lutherans did not. Charles viewed their action as evidence of sedition. For a time it looked as if the diet would be suspended or postponed, but Charles entered the city with the usual imperial fanfare and the diet proceeded on course.

Later the papal emissary proposed a Corpus Christi procession in Augsburg. In the procession, the host, or bread, from the altar was lead through the streets. Those faithful to the pope believed that once a priest consecrated the bread, it became and remained the body of Christ. Reverence for the host, in their view, therefore meant reverence for Christ. But the Lutheran delegation did not participate. They taught that the Sacrament of the Altar was Christ's body and blood to eat and drink for the forgiveness of sins. The host was still bread before and after that. They chose to confess their faith by their action. But their confession of God's truth, while bold, was another example, at least in the eyes of Charles and the others, of their lack of loyalty to the empire and the Roman Church.

The reformed preachers in Augsburg also distressed Charles. He chose to silence them, and issued an order that they cease their worship and preaching. George of Brandenburg objected and said he would rather lose his head than deny God and worship in a way he believed to be false. The emperor responded, "Not head off! Not head off!" (Schaff 7, 698). Charles then silenced the preachers of both parties except those he approved. Luther urged the delegation to abide by the emperor's will. So the Protestants held services in private homes to avoid direct violation of the emperor's directive.

June 25, 1530

These events confirmed the earlier plan by the Lutheran delegation to present a peaceful, positive confession. Melanchthon began working on the confession in May while at Augsburg. Luther received a copy of the work in mid-May and praised it. Melanchthon finished the German version by June 15. But one more step was necessary. The confession also needed to be translated into Latin, the international language of scholars and diplomacy. Both versions of the *Augsburg Confession* were completed for the formal presentation on June 25, 1530.

Considering the previous incidents involving the Lutheran delegation, some feared there might be an uproar and potential riot at the reading of the *Confession*. To minimize that possibility and limit attendance, they chose the bishop's residence, where there was a smaller auditorium for the Protestant presentation.

There the *Confession* would be read aloud in the presence of the emperor and the entire Diet. June of 1530 was unusually warm; the windows had to remain open in the smaller auditorium. The Lutherans took advantage of the situation and chose Christian Beyer to read the *Confession* because of his booming voice. For two hours Beyer read the German version of it. But the smaller auditorium could not contain his voice. The crowds gathered at the windows and heard every word.

What Did These Men Confess?

June 25, 1530, was a memorable day for the Lutheran delegation. Their confession set before the emperor and those attending the Diet what they believed in a calm and clear way. First, they assured the emperor and the others that they were "prepared to discuss, in a friendly manner, all possible ways and means by which we may come together. . . . We will do this in the presence of your Imperial Majesty . . . [so that] dissensions may be put away without offensive conflict. . . . We ought to confess the one Christ and do everything according to God's truth" (11). It was exactly the tone the emperor had sounded in his call to the Diet back in January.

What Melanchthon wrote and Christian Beyer read confessed what the Protestants believed the church had believed at the time of the apostles and for about the first 1,000 years of its existence. They protested the decrees and ordinances that contradicted the apostles and prophets and desired to return the church to its roots in the Old and New Testament. Each article cited Scripture as proof for their thinking. They confessed the truth about God, original sin, the Son of God, justification, ministry, the church, and the sacraments, among other things. One bishop is said to have stated privately, "This is the pure truth. We cannot deny it" (AE 49, 350). Luther in Coburg wrote to Melanchthon after rereading the *Confession,* "I am tremendously pleased with it" (AE 49, 343).

The critical issue was how a sinner becomes right with God. They confessed, "Our churches teach that people cannot be justified before God by their own strength, merits, or works. People are freely justified for Christ's sake, through faith, when they believe that they are received into favor and that their sins are forgiven for Christ's sake. By his death, Christ made satisfaction for our sins. God counts this faith for righteousness in his sight" (Article IV).

On August 3, after a long delay, the Roman Catholics read *A Confutation,* or refutation, of the *Confession* as presented by the Lutherans. It cited church decrees and church fathers, without adequate proof from the Scriptures. The Catholics required the Lutherans to agree with their position but would not submit a copy of their refutation to the Lutherans unless they first agreed to it. The Lutherans remained steadfast. Charles initiated a series of negotiations to seek a solution, but that attempt collapsed on August 30. The emperor informed the reformers that the questions of faith would be decided by a council and until then demanded that the old practices be restored. The emperor acted on the belief that the Lutheran *Confession* was thoroughly refuted by the *A Confutation* but gave "the Elector of Saxony, the five Princes, and the six Cities a time of grace from now until the 15th day of April next year in which to consider whether or not they will confess the other articles together with the Christian Church, His Holiness the Pope, His Imperial Majesty, the other Electors, Princes, and Estates of the Holy Roman Empire . . . until a general council shall be convoked" (Schwiebert 734).

Before the Diet recessed, Melanchthon began work on a defense, or apology, of their confession at Augsburg—the Lutheran answer to *A Confutation.* He had no written copy of the Catholic document but based his work on the notes of *A Confutation* made by stenographers. A version of it was ready before he left the Diet. But when the Lutherans offered Charles their response, his brother, Ferdinand, whispered that he should not accept it. So Charles refused. But Melanchthon's work was not forgotten. His revision of the response would be ready by the deadline set for compliance by the Diet and eventually become the *Apology of the Augsburg Confession.*

Later, Luther wrote, "Christ has been proclaimed through this public, glorious confession, and has been affirmed in bright daylight and in the very presence of these [opponents], so that they may not boast that we have run away, have been afraid, or have hidden our faith. I only envy you this opportunity, for I could not be present at this [time when] the beautiful confession [was presented]" (AE 49, 368).

While all this was going on in Augsburg, Luther awaited impatiently for information at Coburg. The letters came sporadically. While he waited for news, he worked. What was he doing? ❦

NORTH SEA

1530

BALTIC SEA

MAY 29, 1530

Luther's father, Hans, dies.

SEP 23, 1530

Elector John leaves Diet of Augsburg.

Wittenberg

London

CHRISTMAS 1530

Philip of Hesse helps form the Smalcald League to defend Lutherans.

ENGLISH CHANNEL

Coburg

Nuremberg

Augsburg

JUL 23, 1532

Peace of Nuremberg joins Catholics and Lutherans against Turks.

AUG 16, 1532

John Frederick the Magnanimous becomes elector of Saxony.

ADRIATIC SEA

SEP 7, 1533

Elizabeth, future queen of England, born.

Rome

1535

MEDITERRANEAN SEA

CHAPTER FIFTEEN

NUREMBERG, GERMANY

JULY 23, 1532

Before leaving for Augsburg in early February 1530, Luther's brother James reported that their father, Hans, was seriously ill. Luther was worried about his father and wanted to see him but explained that the weather and the personal danger of his travel made it impossible to visit. The letter he wrote on February 15 to his father testifies to Luther's deep feelings for his father and his deep faith in God's promises in the face of death. He offered his father and mother the opportunity to come to Wittenberg to live, telling them, "It would be a great joy for me . . . if it were possible for you and mother to be brought here to us; this my Katie, too, desires with tears. . . . It would be a heartfelt joy for me (as would be only right) to be around you in person and to show, with filial faithfulness and service, my gratitude to God and to you." But that was not possible, so Luther commended his father to God, "who loves you more than you love yourself. . . . Our faith is certain, and we don't doubt that we shall shortly see each other again in the presence of Christ. . . . It is only a matter of an hour's sleep, and all will be different" (AE 49, 268-71). The letter was circulated among Luther's friends and found a home in the hearts of many over the years who had to confront the loss of a loved one.

In other matters, Luther's attention turned to the issue of armed resistance to the emperor and the Roman Catholics. Luther strongly advised against such a policy. "It is in no way proper for anyone who wants to be a Christian to stand up against the authority of his government regardless of whether [it] acts rightly or wrongly" (AE 49, 275). His letter (March 6, 1530) to Elector John was circulated among others and eventually found its way into the hands of Luther's opponents, who used it against the Lutheran resistance to Catholic uniformity.

Luther at Coburg

While the delegation arrived in Coburg on April 15, they stayed in the city itself. They paused to celebrate Easter there. Nine days later, the night before the elector left for Augsburg, Luther entered the Veste (Fortress) Coburg secretly in the night to avoid any demonstration. He spent a sleepless night scouting the castle that would be his home while the others attended the Diet. Paul Bader and his wife cared for Luther as part of the staff of 30 that managed the fortress. Luther's secretary, Veit Dietrich, stayed with him at Coburg. Once the others left, Luther was without his familiar routine and camaraderie. He wrote to his friends in jest of watching the "diet" of birds that noisily conducted their sessions of their own diet outside his windows. But he soon longed for a "forest of letters" from those in Augsburg and was frustrated that they did not come more frequently. He threatened to treat his friends with the same silence and isolation he felt. But he relented and wrote letters of encouragement to the elector and others, often to Melanchthon.

He also wrote to Katie back in Wittenberg. She had sent him a picture of their one-year-old daughter, Magdalen—Lenchen as he called her. The picture must have been dark, because at first he did not recognize her, but he put the picture opposite his place at the table in his quarters. To Katie he wondered if the diet would actually get started, since the emperor was delaying in Innsbruck. He also wondered if there would be some "foul play" (AE 49, 314-5). Luther sent a letter to his son, Hanschen, encouraging him to keep at his studies. The letter is a touching depiction of a pretty, beautiful garden where children who like to pray, study, and be good can come. Luther promised to bring him a nice present when he returned.

If Luther could not be with the delegation at Augsburg, he still made his presence felt. His first work from his separate place among the birds was the *Exhortation to All Clergy Assembled at Augsburg.* It was sent to the printer in Wittenberg on May 12, and 500 copies were delivered to Augsburg on June 7. It quickly sold out, and in spite of the imperial government's injunction not to republish and sell it, sales continued. Luther's friends appreciated his historical review of Reformation events leading up to the Diet included in the *Exhortation.*

Along the way he identified the abuses that needed correction. About confession he wrote, "You have said nothing at all to us about the comfort of absolution, the chief article and the best part in confession, which strengthens faith and trust in Christ. But you have made a work out of it . . ." About penance he wrote, "If one were to forgive and remit all abominations, one can never forgive you for this one. . . . You taught us that we should by our own works make satisfaction for sin, even against God. And that was called repenting of sin. You have nowhere given so much emphasis to contrition and confession, although you have made works of them also. Now what else does it mean to say, 'You must make satisfaction for your sins,' than to say, 'You must deny Christ, renounce your baptism . . . disbelieve the forgiveness of sins . . .'? If a conscience is to rely and build on its own works, it stands on loose sand which moves to and fro and continually sinks away" (AE 34, 19-21). He also suggested that the Mass—a sacrifice and offered only to the people in one kind (bread)—was a new doctrine introduced after the apostles and was contrary to the Scriptures. He also cited other doctrines that were new doctrines unknown to the apostles.

Finally, he asked simply to be allowed to proclaim the message of the gospel: "Allow us to teach the gospel freely and let us serve the poor people who desire to be pious. . . . We wish to let you remain as you are and teach (as we have done in the past) that you should be allowed to be princes and lords, for the sake of peace, and that your properties should be left alone. . . . We will perform the duties of your office; we will support ourselves without cost to you; we will help you remain as you are; and we will counsel that you have authority and are to see to it that things go right" (AE 34, 49-50).

While at Coburg, Luther received a letter that informed him of his father's death. The news upset him. "This death has certainly thrown me into sadness, thinking not only of nature, but also of the very kind love [my father had for me]; for through him my Creator has given me all that I am and have." For two days Luther mourned. In his letter to Melanchthon he concluded, "For it is right and God-pleasing for me, as a son, to mourn such a father, from whom the Father of [all] mercies has brought me forth, and through whose sweat [the Creator] has fed and raised me to whatever I am. Indeed I rejoice that he has lived till now so that he could see the light of truth" (AE 49, 319).

When letters came with the news of the reading of the *Augsburg Confession* before the Diet, he wrote, "I am tremendously pleased to have lived to this moment when Christ, by his staunch confessors, has publically been proclaimed in such a great assembly by means of this really most beautiful confession" (AE 49, 354). He may have been a bit disappointed that Melanchthon wrote so tactfully in the confession—"stepped so softly" he said. Yet the two reformers were of different temperaments. Luther was bold and direct; Melanchthon was quiet, resolute, and irenic. In spite of their difference in style there was little difference in substance at this point, and this was a momentous event for the Lutherans, for the church, and for the ages.

Luther's Seal

The symbol identified as Luther's seal makes an appearance while Luther was at Coburg. Some evidence suggests that the coat of arms had developed much earlier. Its origins are not clear and it seems that Luther may have developed the seal by adapting his own family's coat of arms. But at this point, the elector ordered that Luther's rose be made into a beautiful stone. Either a drawing or the seal itself was presented to Luther in the castle. He wrote this explanation of the seal:

> There is first to be a cross, black in a heart, which should be of its natural color, so that I myself would be reminded that faith in the Crucified saves us. For if one believes from the heart he will be justified. Even though it is a black cross, which mortifies and also should hurt us, yet it leaves the heart in its natural color and does not ruin nature; that is, the cross does not kill but keeps one alive. For the just man lives by faith, but by faith in the Crucified One. Such a heart is to be in the midst of a white rose, to symbolize that faith gives joy, comfort, and peace; in a word it places the believer into a white joyful rose; for this faith does not give peace and joy as the world gives and, therefore, the rose is to be white and not red, for white is the color of the spirits and of all the angels. Such a rose is to be in a sky-blue field, symbolizing that such joy in the Spirit and in faith is a beginning of the future heavenly joy; it is already a part of faith, and is grasped through hope, even though not yet manifest. And around this field is a golden ring, symbolizing that in heaven such blessedness lasts forever and has no end, and in addition is precious beyond all joy and goods, just as gold is the most valuable and precious metal (AE 49, 358-9).

Luther let his beard grow again as he had done in the Wartburg. In September, when he was reunited with his friends, Elector John had difficulty recognizing him. It also seems that Luther may have had difficulty seeing clearly and needed glasses, but the glasses he received were more trouble than help. He did have health issues. Among other things, he complained to Katie of throbbing in his head, headaches, and dizziness. Yet he sought to assure her that he was healthy and pointed to the number of things he had written while away from her.

The negotiations that followed the reading of the *Confession* seemed an endless delay of the inevitable. The Lutherans rejected the *Confutation* presented by the Roman Catholics. It was revised by the emperor's order several times before its presentation. Afterward, he directed negotiations to find a resolution. Luther felt that all that could be done was done and that no concessions could be made. He wrote to the delegation in Augsburg, "You will have to hear 'fathers, fathers, fathers, church, church, church, usage, custom.' Moreover you will hear nothing taken from Scripture. . . . Do not hope for unity or concessions" (AE 49, 374-6).

In Luther's view the emperor had three options. He could insist that the Edict of Worms be strictly enforced. He could submit the *Augsburg Confession* to a panel of nonpartisan scholars for evaluation and then pass judgment. The third option was for the emperor to decree that the status before Augsburg be restored until a universal council could be convened. Luther was impatient for the delegation to leave Augsburg and head home. He advised, "In the name of the Lord I free you from this diet. Home, and again, home! . . . Our case has been made, and beyond this you will not accomplish anything better or more advantageous. . . . Home, home!" (AE 49, 376-7). But months passed before the delegation left Augsburg and returned to familiar and friendly Wittenberg.

The Lutheran delegation was not the only group concerned about losing its status in the empire because they protested abuses in the Roman Church. Two other confessions by other reformation groups were also presented at Augsburg. The first was a confession by the Reformed Church in Germany called the Tetrapolitan Confession—a confession of four imperial cities. It was not accepted by the diet. The second was the confession of Zwingli, but it too was rejected. Both were treated with contempt and were not allowed to be read to the Diet.

After *A Confutation* was read and all negotiations failed, Emperor Charles V pronounced that the Lutheran position was refuted. The Lutherans again protested claiming that *A Confutation* did not refute their beliefs. From his perspective, Charles took an expected position against the Protestants and gave them until April 15, 1531, to comply or face the consequences—the enforcement of the Edict of Worms so long delayed. But, interestingly, Charles also promised to call a general council so that the religious issues could be settled. Some Roman Catholics—Charles included—still felt the need for necessary reforms and that a church council was one way to achieve them.

Theological and Political Defense

On September 23 the emperor granted Elector John permission to leave the Diet. Luther wrote to Katie informing her that he hoped to be home in two weeks. On the walls of his chambers he left behind quotations from the psalms placed there for his own comfort. One of the most prominent was Psalm 118:17: "I will not die but live, and will proclaim what the LORD has done." Luther did more than write on the walls; he also sent much to the printers while isolated from his colleagues. For example, he wrote about the education of children in *A Sermon on Keeping Children in School.* He wrote commentaries on selected psalms and the Magnificat. He also spent time translating some of the books of the Old Testament into German and revising the translation of Old Testament books already completed—a work that had been underway since the appearance of the New Testament in 1522.

Once back in Wittenberg two issues became urgent—one theological and the other political. The theological issue was the revision of the *Apology* that Melanchthon had worked on while in Augsburg. The deadline set by Charles required a response or submission to the emperor and to *A Confutation* and the Roman Church. After Melanchthon finally received a copy of *A Confutation,* he began rewriting the *Apology* he had drafted while in Augsburg. Luther offered many suggestions for its revision, and the other theologians in Wittenberg also contributed. A revised copy of Melanchthon's personal confession and refutation of the Roman Catholic *Confutation* was ready on April 15, 1531, the date of the emperor's deadline. The *Apology* became the Lutheran response to his ultimatum. Clearly the Lutherans would not submit to the beliefs of the emperor or Rome. The *Apology* is the longest and most detailed confession of the Lutheran confessions and soon gained equal status with the *Augsburg Confession* as a standard for Lutherans.

The second issue was political. Enforcement of the Edict of Worms had been delayed since 1521 because Charles faced opposition from Francis and, at times, the pope. The Turks under Suleiman the Magnificent were still another factor. Now it appeared that only the Turks challenged Charles. Francis I was defeated and the pope humiliated into submission. The Lutherans wondered if Charles would take military action against them in spite of their peaceful tone in the *Augsburg Confession.* Earlier, Luther and the others advised against armed resistance to the emperor, but the tone changed a bit after Augsburg. They still did not wish to authorize rebellion, but self-defense was another thing. In addition, the Lutheran lawyers imagined a scenario where armed resistance to the emperor was necessary if he acted against imperial law and with flagrant injustice.

Philip of Hesse and Elector John of Saxony called a meeting in Smalcald to explore a defensive league. An agreement emerged in 1531. The Smalcald League included eight princes and eleven cities. With the *Augsburg Confession* as the charter, they agreed that if one member was attacked because of their faith, the other members would unite and support them. But it was more than just posturing for the benefit of Charles and the Catholics. They agreed to provide troops—10,000 infantry and 2,000 cavalry split among the members of the league—for their mutual defense.

As April 15 approached, Charles faced his own political difficulties. His plans for the council to settle the religious question were not going well, and the Turks were a growing challenge. He wrote to his wife, Isabella, in July 1531, "I have had to postpone some of my plans this year, for I had hoped that some decision about a council might be reached, since the weal of Christendom hangs on it. But the pope and the Most Christian King are still making difficulties which imperil the whole business. The postponement of the Council has had the worst effect in Germany. The Turkish menace has increased so much that I have even considered coming to an agreement with the Lutherans in order to prevent worse disaster" (Brandi 325). Yes, the Turks had not disappeared. Suleiman planned to make another advance against Vienna. Barbarossa was raiding Christian trade in the Mediterranean. Charles could not risk a civil war in Germany, a very real possibility if he were to enforce the decisions so ominously announced in Augsburg.

He changed policy and began to court the Protestants in order to confront the Turks. The Lutherans responded positively. Luther endorsed the Lutheran participation in a letter to Duke Joachim of Brandenburg, who was the captain of one of the contingents. Luther wrote, "Thus, above all else, I wish and I pray God through Jesus Christ, our Lord, to give the devout Emperor, all the sovereigns, and all those who are now to fight against the Turks, first of all, a courageous heart that relies cheerfully on God's help" (AE 50, 70).

The new policy of Charles became official with the Peace of Nuremberg on July 23, 1532, signed by Catholics and Protestants. Among some, the willingness of the Lutherans to join forces against a common foe raised the estimation of the Lutherans as loyal subjects. Late in summer of 1532, Lutherans and Catholics joined to campaign against the Turks. But the great battle against the Turks never really materialized. The imperial army arrived after Suleiman withdrew. They fought and defeated the Turkish rear guard but could not be encouraged to pursue the Turks. Weather and money were among the reasons that prevented their further advance.

The agreement of Nuremberg also stipulated that a temporary peace would prevail in the empire until a council or national assembly could deal with the religious issues. It also prohibited any armed conflict over faith or other issues. Religious peace—even if temporary—was welcome. In fact, the peace would persist until after Luther's death, but the Nuremberg agreement would not remove the tension between Catholics and Protestants. ❦

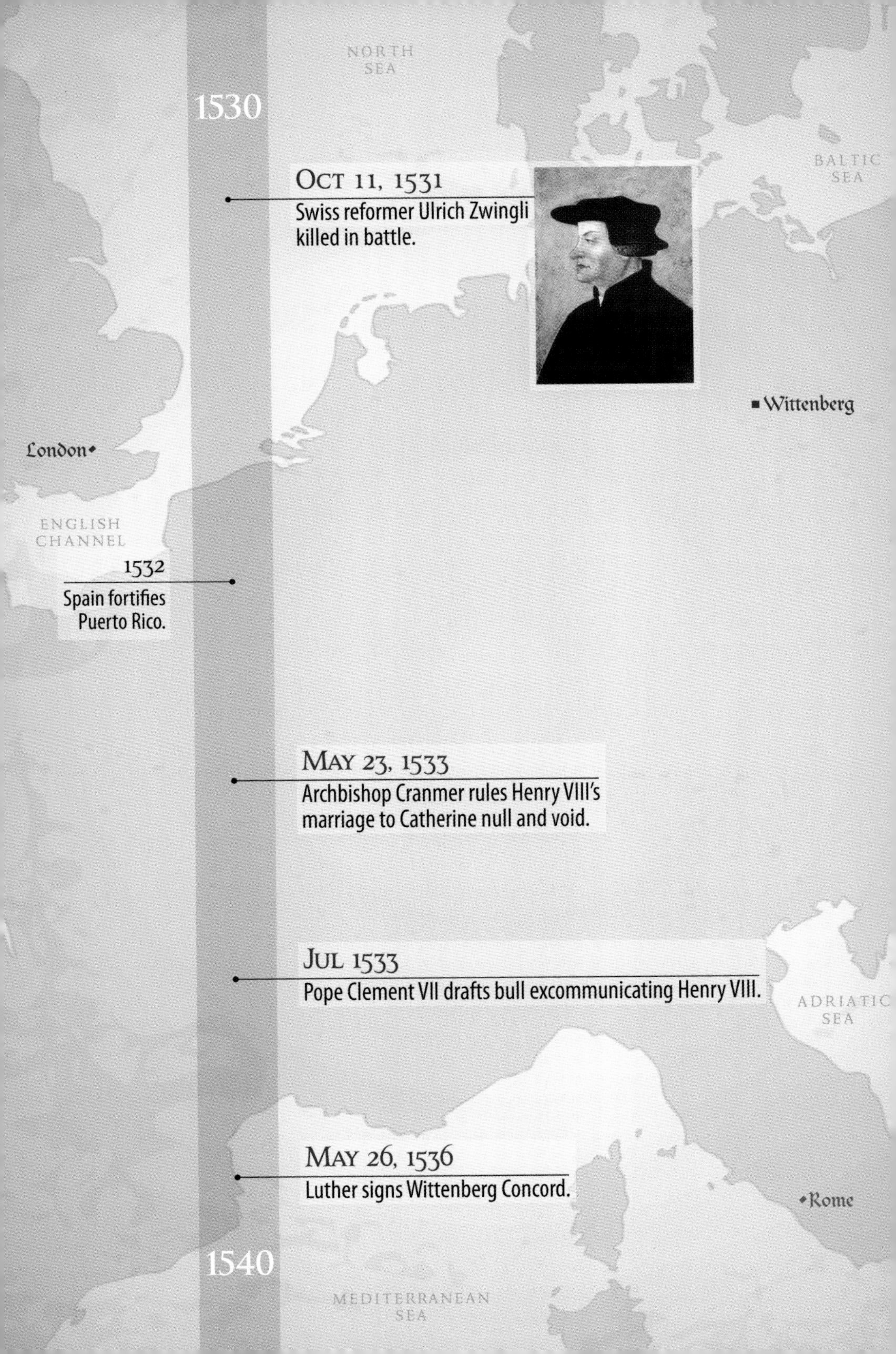

1530

OCT 11, 1531

Swiss reformer Ulrich Zwingli killed in battle.

1532

Spain fortifies Puerto Rico.

MAY 23, 1533

Archbishop Cranmer rules Henry VIII's marriage to Catherine null and void.

JUL 1533

Pope Clement VII drafts bull excommunicating Henry VIII.

MAY 26, 1536

Luther signs Wittenberg Concord.

1540

NORTH SEA

BALTIC SEA

Wittenberg

London

ENGLISH CHANNEL

ADRIATIC SEA

Rome

MEDITERRANEAN SEA

CHAPTER SIXTEEN

WITTENBERG, GERMANY

MAY 29, 1536

Those who confessed their faith in Augsburg on June 25, 1530, adopted Psalm 119:46 as the motto for their *Confession:* "I will speak of your statutes before kings and will not be put to shame." They did indeed speak before kings—Charles and Ferdinand—and did so respectfully to the imperial government of Charles. The preface to the *Confession* sounded the tone, stating, "in compliance with the wish of Your Imperial Majesty . . . in dutiful obedience to Your Imperial Majesty, as our most gracious Lord . . ." The confessors also acknowledged the threat of the Turks, quoting the invitation to the Diet and its purpose to deliberate concerning "the Turks, that hereditary foe of ours and of the Christian name." The preface concluded with references to the council Charles promised to persuade the Roman pontiff to call. They pledged "to prepare for such a Christian, free, general council and to plead for it. . . . We also have, following legal form and procedure, called upon and appealed to such a council and to Your Imperial Majesty at various times concerning these most important matters" as they had done at the second Diet of Speyer in 1529.

The Protestants—Lutheran and others—had come to Augsburg seeking legal recognition and protection under imperial law. It was an important protection for them to seek. In the mind of most, a loyal citizen of the state could not hold a religious conviction different from the state-sanctioned religion. Church and state were intertwined. Conformity to the Roman Church was the same as loyalty also to the state. Divergence from the Roman Catholic rule of faith was insubordination and insurrection. There were legal and political questions to settle. Were Lutherans, the "Protestants," loyal to the state or were they similar to the radical Anabaptists? Should they be opposed by force of arms for the sake of political order and stability? Were they rebels? Freedom of religion was not yet a dominant thought in either the minds of the church or the state. And the distinction of the two kingdoms—church and state—was only slowly emerging. Luther was one voice sounding a different approach; other voices had also been raised. Yet in the real world of German princes and imperial politics, the idea was still muddled.

The Augsburg Confession sought to identify those who signed it as reformers of the one faith handed down from the apostles and prophets, freeing it from the traditions that had distorted the simple faith of the early Christians. The Confession also wanted to remind Charles that, in spite of their differences with the Roman Church, the Lutherans were loyal subjects of the state.

The Confession pointedly condemned the Anabaptists (Augsburg Confession Article XVI), because the Anabaptists abandoned allegiance to all governmental authority. The Zwickau prophets, Thomas Muntzer, and the bloody Peasants' Revolt were all part of the consciousness of the age. The Anabaptists were deemed too radical for either Roman Catholics or Lutherans and were persecuted by both. But the movement could not be wiped out. After the Peasants' Revolt, Menno Simons (1496–1561) led the Anabaptists away from the violence of the first radical tenets because he believed they were not scriptural. The Anabaptists nevertheless rejected the Roman Catholic Church and focused instead on separation of church and state and works of love and concern for others. Today the Mennonites trace their origins to Simons' reformation of the Anabaptist early radicalism.

The emperor's response at Augsburg was the ultimatum that all must comply with Roman Catholic teaching by April 15, 1531. But the policy shifted in the face of Suleiman's plans for a Muslim Europe. Lutherans showed their loyalty to the state without abandoning their confession. Charles made good on his pledge to persuade the pope to call a council. It did not bear fruit during the reign of Clement VII, but Charles persisted after Clement died. Some Catholics still believed that the "heretics" should be subdued by force. Charles had not completely abandoned the use of force against the "heretics," but he had only set it aside to deal with the Turks. In the meantime, the Protestants did not neglect the idea of preparing to defend their faith and territory, even if it meant armed conflict.

Unity Among Reformers

One of the most significant events during these years was the agreement between the southern German cities and Luther over the Lord's Supper. The discussions came with baggage from earlier discussions. Even before the

Augsburg Diet, Phillip of Hesse recognized that those who sought to reform the church should be drawn together and form a united front. He called Luther and Zwingli and their colleagues to Marburg to discuss their differences. In early October 1529, the opposing delegations met in a room of the castle in Marburg to discuss their differing positions.

But the result was only a partial agreement. The critical disagreement was on the Lord's Supper and the interpretation of the words of institution. After this disagreement reached an impasse, Luther proposed a compromise that was also rejected. Finally, Philip, the sponsor of the meeting, asked Luther to draw articles of agreement and disagreement. They are known as the Marburg Articles. In the discussion of these articles the single obstacle to unity was the differing views of the Lord's Supper. Representatives of both sides signed 14 of the articles. The 15th article on the Sacrament remained unsigned.

Less than a year later, the Diet of Augsburg brought the reformers—including those representing the two sides at Marburg—before the imperial court. The Lutherans and the Augsburg Confession achieved a measure of recognition as Christian Beyer read the Confession. The other confessions—Zwingli's *Ratio Fidei* and the Tetrapolitan Confession—were dismissed. With that dismissal any hope of recognition and legal status also disappeared. The four cities that submitted the Tetrapolitan Confession—Strasbourg, Constance, Memmingen, and Lindau—took a position between Lutheran and Zwinglian views of the Lord's Supper. Martin Bucer, once a part of the Wittenberg reformers, was serving in Strasbourg. He attended the diet in Augsburg and sought to find agreement between the two opposing views on the Lord's Supper. He also visited Luther at Coburg, but the illusive agreement did not materialize.

Zwingli continued to oppose the Lutherans as well as the Catholics. His statue in Zurich depicts him with Bible in one hand and sword in the other. The sword is not simply symbolic, representing the sword of the Spirit (Ephesians 6:17). Zwingli did, in fact, swing the sword in battle and died on October 9, 1531, at the hands of the Swiss Catholics, who defeated Zurich's Protestant forces. Nevertheless, his ideas continued to be a force in Switzerland. His death did not necessarily heighten the concern the other reformers had about Roman Catholic military action against Protestants. It did, however, illustrate that their fear of military opposition was justified.

Unity against potential opposition was important for Protestants and especially for Lutherans. That unity was about to take a step forward. Martin

Bucer and Melanchthon had come to a cautious understanding at Augsburg. At first Melanchthon was suspicious of Bucer. Once a trusted translator in Wittenberg, Martin Bucer lost the trust of the Wittenberg reformers. He had inserted Zwinglian views of the Lord's Supper into some of the works of the Wittenbergers he translated. Those insertions were included in some of the works that Luther wrote. He came to Marburg on the side of Zwingli, and when Luther saw him, Luther wagged his finger at him and said, "You rascal." But after Augsburg, Bucer claimed to have changed his mind and, at least, had convinced Melanchthon his switch was genuine. In the years that followed, Bucer wrote and published a number of works that spoke of the Sacrament in the same way as the Wittenberg reformers.

Yet the atmosphere between the two camps was not happy. Luther's polemic was not a positive invitation to discussion and neither was the attitude on the other side. Yet Bucer and Melanchthon sought ways to cool the rhetoric, while each side remained suspicious of the other. Persistence paid off. On April 11, 1536, Luther wrote to invite the southern German theologians to a meeting at Eisenach in order to discuss the differences and seek a solution.

When the representatives of the southwestern cities arrived at Eisenach, Luther was not there. They waited a few days, but instead of turning back they went on to Wittenberg. At Gotha, they learned that Luther was ill. They continued toward Wittenberg and arrived on Sunday evening, May 21, 1536. But the atmosphere continued to be filled with suspicion and ill will like a fog preventing clear vision. Luther had read a recent collection of Zwingli's letters with a complementary preface by Bucer. To Luther, it appeared that Bucer had not really abandoned Zwingli's ideas. Bucer explained that the preface had been written years earlier and the publisher had used it without his consent. That opened the door for dialog, and the discussion lasted late into the night; the fog began to lift. Luther was too ill to move about freely and sat in an armchair.

The suspicion was not completely removed, but the discussions the next day helped. And the following day Luther felt better, and Bucer again admitted that he had been in error about the Lutheran position on the Lord's Supper. He assured Luther that he had changed his views. When he explained his new position, Luther was impressed. But Luther wanted to make sure that the entire delegation shared that belief. The southern German delegation confessed that they had been teaching the scriptural position in their congregations for over a year. They had further accepted the *Augsburg Confession* and the *Apology*. It was a great step forward.

The Lutherans withdrew to another room to discuss this development. They decided that one more question needed a response: did the unworthy actually receive the body of Christ when they receive the bread. The Lutheran theologians wanted to be faithful to the Scriptures and remove any doubt that the delegation from the south still retained a symbolic view that the bread and wine only represented the body and blood. So they returned from the caucus and put the question to the others. The southern German reformers readily agreed that the unworthy received the body of Christ. There was agreement and unity on the Sacrament. Exultation and tears of joy followed. The two sides celebrated the unity with the hand of Christian fellowship.

A joint service with Holy Communion soon followed, and Melanchthon was given the task of preparing a report. Luther and the others signed the agreement Melanchthon drafted on May 26, 1536. It came to be called the Wittenberg Concord, and it ended the bitterness, suspicion, and doubt evident at first. The southern reformers were to return to their congregations and work to extend the unity they had achieved in Wittenberg. They worked to achieve unity there, but not all the Reformation groups eventually agreed with the Concord. Some of Zwingli's followers remained unconvinced and unmoved. They would later find that the Swiss reformer, John Calvin, expressed views of the Sacrament that they could accept. But the Wittenberg reformers embraced Bucer and the others who moved away from Zwingli's position of symbolic interpretation of the Lord's Supper and closer to the Wittenberg position.

Henry VIII Redux as a Protestant

In 1521 Henry VIII received the title "Defender of the Faith" from Pope Leo X for his attack against Luther. But the political and religious world in England changed. At the time Henry wrote against Luther, Henry was married to Catherine of Aragon, the aunt of Charles V. At age 3, Catherine was betrothed to Henry's brother Arthur. A dozen years later, when Arthur became king of England, he married Catherine, now 15. But Arthur died five months afterward, and his brother Henry became king. Catherine became the ambassador for the Spanish court in England, the first female ambassador in Europe. Her ties to Spain underscore also her ties to Charles V and the Roman Catholic Church. Henry, shortly after becoming king, married Catherine.

As king of England, Henry played a role in the early Reformation history on the Roman Catholic side. He was an ally of Charles and even planned a joint campaign against Francis. But France and England were not always on opposite sides. At times Emperor Charles stood against them both. The pope first supported the emperor, then opposed him, and finally supported him again. The politics of the Holy Roman Empire always seemed to change. Loyalty was not always the driving force. Instead, each player looked to find his own advantage in the alliances.

But Henry's vision shifted to concentrate on England and its future. He and Catherine had no male heir to inherit his throne. Catherine had one surviving daughter, Mary, and Henry felt that the future required a male heir, especially because Mary was betrothed to the dauphin of France, which eventually could lead to England becoming a province of France. Henry grew determined to separate from his wife Catherine and sire a son. The history of his choices for a wife who would bear him a son ends with Henry on the Protestant side.

The story began when he petitioned Pope Clement VII to annul his marriage to Catherine so he could marry again. Earlier, Pope Julius II had granted Henry dispensation to marry Catherine, his brother's wife, in the first place. Then the marriage was seen as a violation of Leviticus 20:21: "If a man marries his brother's wife, it is an act of impurity; he has dishonored his brother." In spite of the dispensation allowing the marriage, Henry sought a second dispensation to divorce her. Even though requests like Henry's were not unusual, Clement VII was not in a position to grant Henry's request and further anger Charles, Catherine's nephew. He delayed the decision. The request of Henry became a thorny problem for the pope, Charles, and England. The pope's political and military efforts suffered a serious blow when Rome was sacked and pillaged in 1527 by unpaid imperial soldiers. The long negotiations with Charles V afterwards had ended with the coronation of Charles in Bologna in 1530. It would be difficult for Clement to turn against the monarch who had weakened and humiliated him.

With the pope's reluctance evident, Henry sought to avoid the papal negotiations and began to ask the universities of Europe for their opinions for ending his marriage. The University of Wittenberg was among them. Most of the universities approved the proposed annulment of Henry's marriage to Catherine. Luther, however, wrote to Robert Barnes, an English exile who somehow got involved in the issue. In his letter dated September 3, 1531, Luther took the opposite position: "Under no circumstances will he [Henry] be free to divorce the Queen to whom he is married. . . . Before I would approve of such a divorce I would rather permit the King to marry still another woman and to have, according to the examples of the patriarchs and kings, two women or queens at the same time" (AE 50, 32-3). In the long negotiations with the officials in Rome, Cardinal Wolsey suggested the same idea—a second marriage rather than a divorce—as a compromise (Durant, 541).

But history records a different solution. On May 23, 1533, Thomas Cranmer, the Archbishop of Canterbury, ruled that Henry's marriage to Catherine was null and void. Five days later Henry legally—according to English law—married Anne Boleyn, who gave birth to a daughter, Elizabeth. There was still no son and male heir. Anne had three miscarriages and did not give birth to the expected male heir. She was executed in 1536, but her daughter Elizabeth would have a significant role in making England Protestant in the future. Henry married a succession of women in order to father a male heir: Jane Seymour, Anne of Cleves, Catherine Howard, and Katherine Parr.

Pope Clement responded to Henry's marriage to Anne by excommunicating Henry and stripping from him the title "Defender of the Faith," which Leo had bestowed and Clement himself had confirmed on him. England did not kneel in obedience. The English Parliament passed the Act of Supremacy in 1534. It stated, "By authority of this present Parliament . . . the king, our sovereign lord, and his heirs and successors, kings of this realm shall be taken, accepted, and reputed the only supreme head on earth of the Church of England, called Anglicans Ecclesia." The act acknowledged that Henry and the English had abandoned the pope and the Roman Catholic Church. The act was repealed in 1554 by Henry's Roman Catholic daughter Mary, who later became queen, but a second Act of Supremacy was passed in 1559 when Elizabeth, a Protestant, ascended to the throne of England.

Henry's shift to the Protestant side was clearly not one of conviction and teaching. It was political. On one level it was motivated by the desire to escape his marriage to Catherine so that he could marry Anne Boleyn. On another level it was a desire to secure England as a nation independent from the Holy Roman Empire and the Hapsburgs, the family of Charles. Once the decision to abandon Rome was made, Henry looked for allies that would help maintain England's independence. One effort was to send delegations to Saxony in Germany and the Smalcald League. The League was obviously antipapal, and Henry had set England against the pope and Rome when Parliament passed the Act of Supremacy. The English requested that Melanchthon visit England. But Elector John Frederick would not let him go. In these negotiations and others the German reformers maintained a theological focus on teaching the Scriptures while others approached issues politically.

France

France was officially Roman Catholic. Yet the ongoing conflict with Charles drove them also to approach John Frederick and ask for Melanchthon to come to France. The elector also refused that request. Protestant influence in France would not come from the Germans and Luther. The influence came from French speaking Switzerland and John Calvin. Eventually the Huguenots, French Protestants, grew and posed a threat to the Roman Catholic majority. Tension between Protestants and Catholics grew as it did all over Europe. In these events, the religious issues were gradually slipping from the primary concern of kings and kingdoms. Political and national issues began to muscle their way ahead of the religious. Nationalism was emerging as a force for France and England, as well as for Germany.

At this time France was seeking allies to oppose Charles V. It was natural for them to reach out to the Smalcald League since the League was created as a defense against potential military action by Charles V and the pope. But their discussion with the Germans produced little. France, however, took a bold and unexpected step as it sought to continue its struggle against Charles. They made contact with the Turks and Suleiman the Magnificent. The contact with the Muslims was a scandal in Europe and considered a sacrilegious alliance. Today it is considered one of the first nonideological diplomatic unions between a Christian and non-Christian empire. The alliance provided both the Turks and Francis I resources to fight against Charles.

1530

1534
Entire Bible published in German.

1534
Ignatius Loyola forms Society of Jesus (Jesuits).

SEP 25, 1534
Clement VII dies.

OCT 13, 1534
Paul III becomes pope; takes steps to call a council.

1536
John Calvin publishes first edition of *Institutes*.

1537
Luther prepares the Smalcald Articles. Elector John Frederick remains firm in his faith.

1537
Melanchthon drafts *Treatise on the Power and Primacy of the Pope* in preparation for general council.

SEP 28, 1538
Battle at Preveza: Barbarossa with Turkish fleet defeats Spanish.

1540

1535

Dec 17, 1538
Paul III issues 1533 bull excommunicating Henry VIII.

May 4, 1540
Venice and Turks sign Treaty of Constantinople.

Dec 12, 1545
Council of Trent convened.

Feb 18, 1546
Luther dies in Eisleben. Martin Luther, Reformer, 1483–1546.

1546
Beginning of Smalcald War.

1550

NORTH SEA
BALTIC SEA
Wittenberg
London
Eisleben
ENGLISH CHANNEL
ADRIATIC SEA
Rome
MEDITERRANEAN SEA

CHAPTER EIGHTEEN

EISLEBEN, GERMANY

FEBRUARY 18, 1546

A month after Luther left Smalcald near death with kidney stones, he was still feeling its effects. He wrote to his long-time friend George Spalatin on March 21, 1537: "By God's grace I gradually recuperate, and learn to eat and drink again. Yet my thighs, knees, and bones are still shaky, and are thus far not sufficiently strong to carry my body. I am more exhausted than I thought, but I shall take care of myself with rest and other nourishment until through God's help I have regained my strength" (AE 50, 170).

His recovery, even if it was slow, was good news. For those who had joined Luther in his protest against Rome, he became an oracle as they sought his advice and direction on many things. Of course, the tension between the Lutheran Protestants and the Roman Catholics continued without consideration of Luther's health. The religious divide between them was not resolved but only deferred. A truce of sorts persisted. Some on both sides hoped a universal council would restore unity. Others sought hope by efforts to resolve the differences. Charles V initiated efforts to bring the two sides together. On April 19, 1539, the Truce of Frankfurt assured the Lutherans that the emperor would not take military action against them for 15 months. In the meantime, the two opposing sides were to resolve their differences. At the same time, the Lutherans were expected to support Charles in his war against the Turks in exchange for the truce.

The discussion between the two parties began in Hagenau on August 1 and was later moved to Worms. The discussions at first seemed positive. A genuine discussion on the *Augsburg Confession* took place between Melanchthon and John Eck, but the colloquy was adjourned until the Diet of Regensburg (1541). Luther had remained in Wittenberg while

Melanchthon and others represented the Lutherans. A series of articles representing these discussions were collected in what was called the Regensburg Book. Discussion on the articles continued for some time. Both Charles and the Lutherans desired peace and unity. But eventually no agreement on the key issue—justification by faith—was reached. What was evident already at Augsburg in 1530 was underscored again. No compromise was possible. Only a truce was possible. Others felt differently. Military action by Charles V against the heretics, at some point in the future, was one option still open to the emperor.

An example of the tension that characterized this time comes from Ducal Saxony, the territory of Duke George. From the Leipzig debate onward, George opposed Luther's teachings. He had banned Luther's Bible in his territory and had opposed as often as possible his counterpart in Electoral Saxony for his support of Luther. In spite of his opposition citizens from Ducal Saxony went to hear sermons and receive the Lord's Supper across the border in Electoral Saxony. Duke George responded by ordering surveillance of those crossing the border. In September 1532, 14 citizens of Ducal Saxony refused to return to the Catholic faith. They were expelled.

In Leipzig, Dr. Augustine Sprecht had turned to the Protestant side as well and had refused to receive Holy Communion in only one kind—the bread only (Brecht, *Pres.* 66). He died in Leipzig, but as a Protestant he could not be buried in a Catholic cemetery. He had to be buried in unconsecrated ground. In spite of that, almost the entire city attended his funeral. Duke George forbade any participation in such funerals in the future.

Luther Was Human

In discussion and also on the printed page, Melanchthon was smooth and soft; Luther, on the other hand, was often rough and sometimes painfully pointed. The *Augsburg Confession* is an example of Melanchthon's style. Luther appreciated the work of his colleague at Augsburg, saying that Melanchthon stepped more softly than he could. Luther's writing, on the other hand, had almost always contained a harsh and belligerent tone, especially when he had opposed those who stood against the gospel. In these times of conflict in the 16th century, a war of words meant both sides wrote in the same harsh, belligerent language. If one reviews Luther's writings, one can find some with a much different, much warmer and loving tone, such as *Treatise on Good Works* and *Freedom of a Christian*. Even when reading his sharp and harsh language, Luther's clear focus on the gospel and the truths of Scripture are comforting, enlightening, and powerful enough for readers to gloss over the jagged edges. Some, of course, would not agree with that assessment.

In our age, Luther's tone repels readers. We are always reminded to write and speak without accusations and name-calling. But even in our age, emotions break our restraint and name-calling and crude language sometimes prevail in heated arguments and disagreements. When Luther opposed those who would not believe that Jesus was the sole source of comfort before God, he had no desire to withhold his frustration. It broke out in a torrent of harsh words. It was indeed a war of words and often a hot war of words.

One of those torrents was directed at the Jews. Luther has been accused of inciting anti-Semitism. Words warning the Jews and the Catholics of the consequences of rejecting Jesus are not pleasant to hear or read. In the age of Luther, opposition to Jews and Muslims was part of daily life. Ferdinand and Isabella, the king and queen of Spain before Charles, expelled the Jews from their country. They were accorded the title "Catholic King and Queen" by Pope Alexander VI in 1494. The opposition to the Jews spilled over into political and even physical persecution by the Spaniards, but they were prevalent in almost all of Europe. It is a sad chapter in history that, in some ways, has not completely disappeared. Luther need not be excused for his outburst. He was a sinful human like all humans. His focus was first on the doctrines that he opposed. For Luther it was about the teaching of Scripture—the gospel of justification by God's grace through faith in Christ. His excesses and failings are part of history and require first the forgiveness of Christ and then our desire not to repeat or endorse these mistakes or others. In dealing with historical events, we abandon what is wrong but retain what is important and valuable.

Another example of human failure would be Luther's advice to Philip of Hesse. Philip was a vigorous supporter of the Reformation and Luther. He and Elector John Frederick formed the bulwark of the Smalcald League. Yet Philip was not perfect. His marriage was unhappy, and even though the marriage had produced seven children, Philip was nevertheless unfaithful to his wife. His failure troubled his conscience to the point that he avoided receiving Holy Communion. In 1539 he pursued a relationship with a young lady-in-waiting. Her mother would not consent to the relationship unless Philip would agree to a second marriage. Bigamy was against the imperial law and punishable by death.

Philip sought the approval of Luther, Melanchthon, and the elector of Saxony for the second marriage. His argument was that the Old Testament allowed the practice, and that the Wittenbergers, while opposing the divorce of Henry VIII, had advised him to marry a second wife. Luther and the others reluctantly gave their approval to Philip's secret marriage to Margaret von der Saale. They asserted that God intended marriage as a lifelong union of one man and one woman, but there were established precedents for the permission. They wanted the advice kept secret. On March 4, 1540, Margaret and Philip were married. But their marriage did not remain secret, and the situation brought cries of indignation and anger from Catholic enemies of the Reformation. When all the facts were known, it was clear that Luther had not been given the whole truth. When he discovered it, he was furious. It was an unfortunate black eye for Luther and the Reformation. The Reformation lost some credibility, and Philip was hampered by the incident as leader of the Smalcald League.

Luther was not immune to human tragedy. Hardship and trouble are part of human life. Luther and Katie lost a daughter, Elizabeth, who was born on December 10, 1527. Sadly, the Luthers' little daughter did not live to see her first birthday. She died in August of the following year. On May 4, 1529, the Luthers welcomed another daughter, Magdalen. But 13 years later, they endured her death too. She had become so sick that all believed she was near death. Lenchen, as she was called, had become deeply attached to her older brother Hans and asked to see her brother who had gone off to school in Torgau. Martin wrote to the school superintendent to send him home. He wrote, "Magdalen is ill and almost in her last hour; in a short while she might depart to the true Father in heaven, unless God has decreed otherwise" (AE 50, 235). The cause of her illness has never been determined. Hans came home to say good-bye to his sister. She died in her father's arms on September 20, 1542.

Luther wrote to his friend Justus Jonas three days later, "I believe the report has reached you that my dearest daughter Magdalen has been reborn in Christ's eternal kingdom. I and my wife should only joyfully give thanks for such a felicitous departure and blessed end by which Magdalen has escaped the power of the flesh, the world, the Turk, and the devil; yet the force of our natural love is so great that we are unable to do this without crying and grieving in our hearts, or even without experiencing death ourselves. For the features, the words, and the movement of the living and dying daughter who was so very obedient and respectful remain engraved deep in the heart; even the death of Christ (and what is the dying of all people in comparison with Christ's death?) is unable totally to take all this away as it should. You, therefore, please give thanks to God in our stead! For indeed God did a great work of grace to us when he glorified our flesh in this way. Magdalen had (as you know) a mild and lovely disposition and was loved by all" (AE 50, 238).

What Luther did not know at this time was that his own death was less than four years away. In June of 1543 Luther wrote to a friend, "For myself I desire a good hour of passing on to God. I am content, I am tired, and nothing more is in me. Yet see to it that you pray earnestly for me, that the Lord takes my soul in peace. I do not leave our congregations in poor shape; they flourish in pure and sound teaching, and they grow day by day through the ministry of many excellent and most sincere pastors" (AE 50, 242). And a little more than a year later (December 5, 1544) he wrote, "Yes, I am sluggish, tired, cold—that is, I am an old and useless man. I have finished my race; it remains only that the Lord call me to my fathers, and that my body be handed over to decomposition and the worms. I have lived enough, if one may call it living" (AE 50, 245).

But Luther still had strong ideas about a council to settle the religious issue in the empire. When the Council of Trent was finally scheduled for 1545 he wrote, "What kind of a monstrosity this is, I do not understand: the Pope shouts that we are heretics and that we must not have a place in the council; the Emperor wants us to consent to the council and its decrees.... If we now have to consent to such a council, why did we not twenty-five years ago agree with the lord of the councils, the pope, and his bulls? Let the pope first acknowledge that the council is superior to him, and let him listen to the council even if it speaks against him" (AE 50, 266-7).

The Final Journey

In July 1545 Luther traveled to Zeitz to settle a dispute among some of the pastors. He travelled there with his son Hans. From Zeitz he wrote to Katie that he did not want to return to Wittenberg: "I would like to arrange matters in such a way that I do not have to return to Wittenberg. My heart has become cold, so that I do not like to be there any longer. I wish you would sell the garden and field, house and all" (AE 50, 278). The letter was a shock to everyone, but Luther was deeply disappointed with the conditions in Wittenberg and angry at the poor public behavior of its citizens. His concerns were not new, but his desire to leave the city and university was.

The shock of Luther's announcement spurred Elector John Frederick, Melanchthon, and others into action. The elector sent his personal physician, Matthias Ratzeberger, to Melanchthon to confer and approach Luther to change his mind. The physician delivered the elector's personal letter. The mission to convince Luther to return succeeded. Luther traveled to the electoral court in Torgau and then travelled back to Wittenberg.

A second journey took place in the winter. On January 23 Luther left Wittenberg for Eisleben because of another dispute—a bitter family dispute that Luther was asked to arbitrate. The journey was not pleasant. A flood and drifting ice made crossing the Saale River dangerous, and the party waited in Halle until it was safe to go on to Eisleben. They arrived on January 28. The issues separating the parties were difficult, and the personalities not easily persuaded to find a peaceful compromise. Deliberations went on. Luther wrote to Melanchthon and Katie while he was there. To Melanchthon he wrote, "Pray for me that the Lord may bring me back home before I am killed by these battles of the wills" (AE 50, 297). To Katie he wrote, "Dear Katie! We are sitting here allowing ourselves to be tortured. Though we want to leave, it will not be possible for us to do so for eight days (as it looks to me)" (AE 50, 300). She was worried about him, and Luther sought to dispel her fears, writing, "Most holy Mrs. Doctor! I thank you very kindly for your great worry which robs you of sleep. . . . Is this the way you learned the Catechism and the faith? Pray, and let God worry. You have certainly not been commanded to worry about me or about yourself. 'Cast your burden on the Lord, and he will sustain you' " (AE 50, 305-6).

Luther finally wrote that the issues had been mostly settled and that he was looking forward to returning home. But Luther's journey back to Wittenberg would be different than he imagined in his letter. In the evening of February 17, Luther complained of sharp pain in his chest. They gave him hot baths and a massage to improve circulation. At about 9:00 in the evening Luther fell asleep. He awoke about an hour later while everyone was still there and then went to the adjoining bedroom and fell asleep again. He awoke again with sharp chest pains. The attack passed, and Luther fell asleep again, but the third attack was much more severe. The doctors were called but could not stop the inevitable. Jonas asked Luther, "Reverend Father, are you willing to die in the name of the Christ and the doctrine which you have preached?" Luther responded strongly, "Yes!" Then some of those who were there thought Luther fell asleep again. But the doctors were clear. Luther was dead.

The next day, February 19, Luther's funeral was held at St. Andrew's Church, just across the street from where he died and only a short distance from where he was born. John Frederick requested that Luther's body be returned to Wittenberg so he could be buried in the Castle Church. Luther's silent journey back to Wittenberg passed crowds paying their last respects. In Wittenberg, Luther's body entered the Castle Church through the same door on which he had likely nailed the first protest, the *95 Theses.* John Bugenhagen preached the final funeral sermon and Melanchthon gave the eulogy proclaiming that Luther had proclaimed the gospel more beautifully than many others in recent times. Luther was finally laid to rest beneath the floor of the church near the pulpit.

Katie was heartbroken. She could neither eat nor sleep. A few weeks later Katie wrote to her sister-in-law, Christina von Bora, about her grief: "For who would not be sad and afflicted at the loss of such a precious man as my dear lord was? He did great things, not just for a city or a single land, but for the whole world. Therefore I am truly so deeply grieved that I cannot tell a single person of the great pain that is in my heart. I do not understand how I can cope with this. I cannot eat or drink, nor can I sleep. And if I had a principality or an empire and lost it, it would not have been as painful as it is now that the dear Lord God has taken from me this precious and beloved man, and not from me alone but from the whole world" (Brecht, *Pres.* 377-8).

During the last years of Luther's life, the clouds of conflict had been building. Luther had prayed that it would not break into open hostility until he was gone. His wish was granted. It would not take long for conflict between Catholics and Lutherans to become more than a war of words. Charles and the Catholics would initiate the military action threatened by the Edict of Worms in 1521. ❦

Reformation motto: *Verbum Dei Manet in Aeternum* (VDMA), or "The Word of God Remains Forever." This symbol marked the swords and canons used by Lutheran soldiers in the Smalcald War.

NORTH SEA

1545

BALTIC SEA

1546
Michelangelo designs dome for St. Peter's, Rome.

Jan 12, 1547
Council of Trent condemns justification by faith.

Wittenberg

London

Muhlberg

ENGLISH CHANNEL

Apr 24, 1547
Charles V defeats Lutheran forces; captures Elector John Frederick.

Feb 25, 1548
Maurice becomes elector of Saxony.

May 15, 1548
Charles imposes Augsburg Interim.

ADRIATIC SEA

Dec 1548
Leipzig Interim proposed.

Rome

1550

MEDITERRANEAN SEA

CHAPTER NINETEEN

MUHLBERG, GERMANY

APRIL 24, 1547

For as long as Luther was in Wittenberg there were two Saxonys ruled by two lines of the same family—the Ernestine (Electoral) and Albertine (Ducal). Duke George ruled Ducal Saxony for all those years, as one of Luther's most vehement opponents. On the other side of the border was Wittenberg, in Electoral Saxony, where Luther lived and worked. During his lifetime, three Electors ruled Electoral Saxony. The first was Frederick the Wise, who sheltered him in the Wartburg Castle. Frederick died in 1525 and was succeeded by his brother John the Constant, a devout Lutheran who helped rebuild the churches in Saxony according to Lutheran doctrine and practice. In 1532 he was succeeded by his son, John Frederick the Magnanimous, who was a leader in the Smalcald League.

Almost seven years before Luther died, on April 17, 1539, Duke George of Saxony died. When George died, his brother Henry became Duke of Saxony. Henry had become a Lutheran years before. George did not want his Saxon territory to become Lutheran and worked to prevent it. Before he died, George tried to disinherit his brother because of his conversion to the Lutheran faith. He attempted to bequeath the duchy to Ferdinand, Charles V's brother. He failed. Henry became Duke. As a result the two Saxon territories both became Lutheran. They were still separate territories, but now they shared one faith—the Lutheran faith. Henry was 66 years old when he came to power and led his territory into the Lutheran camp. But he ruled only two years.

Henry's son Maurice became Duke of Saxony in 1541. His wife was the daughter of Philip of Hesse. Although Maurice was Lutheran, he chose to participate in the emperor's army against the Sultan and Francis. In addition, he chose not to join the Smalcald League in spite of the urging of his father-in-law, Philip. Tension between the two Saxonys was more than religious. Maurice had little love or respect for John Frederick, the elector of Saxony. Maurice turned toward imperial service with Charles, and he served the emperor honorably and faithfully. Charles noticed his ability and his animosity toward Electoral Saxony and seized the opportunity to use Maurice to continue to serve the empire but also to drive a wedge between the Protestants. Charles dangled the carrot of the electoral honor before Maurice as a reward for his efforts on his behalf in Germany. If the Smalcald League could be defeated, Maurice expected to receive the title of elector now held by John Frederick.

The Council of Trent Begins

In the meantime, to the south in Italy, another drama unfolded. After a number of delays, Paul III issued another call for a council at Trent on November 1, 1542. But not only were the Lutherans opposed, the king of France also forbade the publication of the papal summons in his territory. Only a few Italians were present, and Paul adjourned the meeting. He called for the council to reconvene on March 14, 1545, but the Nineteenth Ecumenical Council of the Christian Church was postponed again until December 13, 1545. *Ecumenical* is an adjective out of place for this council. Henry VIII and the English avoided it. Earlier the Lutherans had returned the invitation issued by Clement VII unopened, and the Eastern church had its own problems living under Turkish rule. Pope Paul III, nearly 80 years old, stayed in Rome but sent three cardinals to represent him. To control the council, only the cardinals, bishops, generals, and abbots could vote. Italian bishops loyal to the papacy dominated, and the pope prepared the issues to be debated.

In Paul III's call, or summons, to the council, he traced the history that led to the council, including the conflict between Charles V and the French. The delay in scheduling the council, he observed, was because it had to be called "in so great a tempest of heresies, discords, and wars." The conditions set by the Lutherans for a free, Christian council in which the Scriptures would be the only arbiter of doctrine was rejected. Paul's summons said flatly that those conditions were "totally irreconcilable with the ordinances of our predecessors, with that of the Apostolic See and the ecclesiastical name, as we have made known in other letters" (Trent 2).

After all the false starts and changes, the council did finally convene. The first session dealt with procedure and scheduled the second session for January 1546. The second session outlined the "manner of living" for those attending. The third session convened on February 4, 1546, and adopted a

"Symbol of Faith" as "the first and sole foundation." That symbol, ironically, was the Nicene Creed that came from the church council called by Constantine and was a standard the Protestants also willingly shared. The fourth session began on April 8, 1546, and its agenda was to determine the standard on which the council would rest its decrees and cannons. The truths of the church, according to the council, "are contained in the written books *and* in the unwritten traditions which, received by the Apostles from the mouth of Christ Himself, or from the Apostles themselves, the Holy Ghost dictating, have come down to us, transmitted as it were from hand to hand. Following, then, the examples of the orthodox Fathers, it receives and venerates with a feeling of piety and reverence all the books of the Old and New Testament, since one God is the author of both; *also the traditions,* whether they relate to faith or to morals, as having been dictated either orally by Christ or by the Holy Ghost, and preserved in the Catholic Church in unbroken succession" (emphasis added, Trent 17). This session also decreed that the approved translation was the Latin Vulgate edition. According to the council, anyone who took a different position on a Bible translation than the one agreed upon by the council, "let him be anathema [cursed]."

Luther's question about authority when he appeared before Cajetan at Augsburg and his desire to be proven wrong only from Scripture at Worms was heard and opposed in no uncertain terms. The Bible *and* tradition were given equal authority. The standard was not Scripture alone. On the dual basis of the Bible and tradition, the subsequent sessions would clarify Roman doctrine and again and again condemn Protestant thought and teaching.

War Against the Heretics

Almost as soon as Luther died, the war against the heretics became a sad reality. Charles planned a campaign against the Smalcald League, but those plans had been frustrated by another war with France that began in 1542. The Treaty of Crepy (1544) brought hostilities between the emperor and France to another cease-fire, or truce. A secret draft of the treaty bound the French king to help Charles in reforming the abuses of the church, support the Council of Trent when it convened, and help bring back the Protestants to the Catholic Church. Lutherans were not the only focus. The treaty also sought to frustrate the Swiss reformation lead by John Calvin in Geneva. If force was necessary to subdue the Protestants, Francis agreed to help Charles against them (Brandi 521).

Charles V hesitated, although he was resolved to take military action. He viewed the action against the Protestants as his duty to God for the unity of the Roman Church and peace in the empire. All seemed to be in his favor. Besides the treaty with France, the pope promised money and soldiers, and the Smalcald League was not fully united. Squabbles among the German princes seemed to forecast an imperial victory. The carrot of becoming elector of Saxony brought Maurice to the battle against the Lutherans on the side of Charles and the Roman Church. On June 19, 1546, Maurice of Saxony signed a pact with the emperor.

Charles understood the need for reform and was an unswerving supporter of the Roman Church. Yet he also was cautiously antipapal. Charles wanted the Council of Trent to avoid doctrinal decisions until after the war and made his intent known to the pope. There were a couple of understandable reasons for his request. First, his forces included Protestant soldiers and allies. Charles was not anxious to force Protestants to fight against other Protestants in order to establish Roman Catholic teachings. Second, he may have thought that the way to unity after the military victory could better be achieved by negotiation and conciliation. Unfortunately, the Council of Trent on January 12, 1547, condemned the doctrine of justification by faith in clear and unequivocal terms. Their action dashed the already slim hope for reform and with it the hope of a unified empire with one faith—a dream of Charles for over 20 years. His representative, Diego de Mendoza, commented that the council was under the tyranny of the papal legates and "Together, the council fathers served only Rome and individually they served only themselves" (Blockmans 95). To add insult, on January 22 the pope recalled his forces from Germany, breaking his promise to Charles.

The war in Germany at first was one of maneuver and tactics with limited clashes. Eventually Charles turned his forces to Saxony. The end was quick and decisive. At Muhlberg the imperial forces were victorious on April 24, 1517. Torgau and Wittenberg quickly came under the control of imperial forces. After the defeat at Muhlberg, Elector John Frederick was presented to the emperor, exhausted and slightly wounded. Charles forced him to kneel, pledge loyalty, and ask for forgiveness. He also deprived him of all his titles and made Maurice the new elector of Saxony.

John Frederick was spared but received no other clemency. He became a prisoner of the emperor for as long as the emperor wished. Philip, the father-in-law of Maurice, surrendered when promised fair treatment. But he too ended the campaign as a prisoner of the emperor. The emperor humiliated both of the leaders of the Smalcald League. Their harsh treatment only fed opposition to the emperor among the Lutherans in Germany.

Augsburg and Leipzig Interims

The Lutherans were beaten but not overcome. The Council of Trent continued, but its work was not yet completed. Actually, it would not finish until 1563, and another general council would not be convened for another 300 years. For now, Charles still sought some way to unify the empire under one religious banner. He assumed that all would agree with the decisions of the council once he had crushed all opposition. He therefore commanded the Lutherans and other Protestants to accept the decrees of Trent. Unity seemed within his grasp.

After arranging for discussions between Catholic and Protestant theologians and anticipating some solution, it became clear that the differences could not be bridged. Catholics refused to accept anything that might hint at Protestantism, and Protestants held a similar but opposite view. On May 15, 1548, Charles took the initiative and on his own issued a decree that became known as the Augsburg Interim. He hoped it would serve as a standard and guide for peace until the Council finished its work. There was to be no dissent. The decree of the emperor further forbade anyone to preach, teach, or write against it.

The Interim allowed the Protestant clergy to retain the right to marry and the right to celebrate the Sacrament in both kinds—wine and bread. However, it was predominantly a Roman Catholic document. Among other things, the Interim authorized the return to Roman customs where they had been abandoned, asserted papal supremacy, and reaffirmed the seven Catholic sacraments. The doctrine of justification by faith alone was not included, in spite of the decree of the Council of Trent over a year earlier.

In some places Charles could enforce the Interim by brute force. In these places, enforcement meant that the people protested with their feet and left the churches empty rather than worship. Those who openly rejected the Interim suffered consequences: imprisonment, banishment, and sometimes execution. Some became fugitives and fled rather than face arrest by Spanish soldiers intent on enforcing the Interim. In other places the Interim was more difficult to enforce. It was simply resisted and rejected.

In all this, Charles had failed to learn what Luther had said very early in his protest: one cannot force the heart to believe. Luther refused to take up arms to advance the gospel and resisted those who sought to do so. Many Lutherans protested in whatever way they could find. Former elector, John Frederick, refused to sign the Interim by saying, "If I should acknowledge and adopt the Interim as Christian and godly, I would have to condemn and deny against my own conscience, knowingly and maliciously, the Augsburg Confession"(Bente 97). The emperor met his refusal by removing Luther's writings and even the Bible from him. John Frederick responded that they were able indeed to deprive him of the books but could not tear what he had learned and treasured from his heart.

Leipzig Interim

In 1530, Melanchthon's work at Augsburg in drafting the *Confession* provided a significant step toward legal recognition for the Lutherans. But Melanchthon considered the *Augsburg Confession* his own personal work. He tinkered with its language, almost always trying to create ways the Protestants of all camps could be united. He introduced language that seemed to allow for Calvin's or Zwingli's view of the sacraments. Luther even chided him for thinking that the *Confession* was his own and not the confession of the church. Melanchthon's tinkering created an alternative version of the *Augsburg Confession* that became known as the Variata. Many of Melanchthon's changes did not seriously influence events at this time, but later they created challenges and lead to the *Formula of Concord,* the last of the Lutheran Confessions (1577). That confession was intended to clarify what Lutherans believed.

After Luther's death, Melanchthon had become the leader in these difficult times. The Lutherans expected his opposition to the Augsburg Interim. At first he was defiantly opposed. He refused to change the doctrine of the Lutheran churches, but his opposition shrank in the face of the emperor's threats. The new elector, Maurice, invited him to draft a compromise document that would please the emperor and the Lutherans. Melanchthon prepared it with the help of the Wittenberg and Leipzig theologians, and on December 22, 1548, the Leipzig Interim was adopted.

But this Interim created more controversy. Charles was pleased with it and believed that he could impose it in other places. The document asserted that many of those practices that Catholics and Lutherans argued over were simply nonessential or adiaphora. Melanchthon and the theologians of Wittenberg and Leipzig suggested that they could retain essential Lutheran teaching by conceding what were nonessential customs and teachings. Unfortunately for the Lutherans, the authors of the Interim spelled out the doctrine of justification in such a way that it allowed for a Catholic interpretation. The Leipzig Interim also required the use of Latin in worship, agreed to seven sacraments, and outlined the observance of Catholic fast and feast days. To no one's surprise, many of the Lutherans felt agreeing to either interim was a denial of

God's truth and a sellout to the Catholics in order to avoid persecution. Melanchthon became an enemy of many who were unwilling to sign away justification by faith and many other Lutheran core teachings.

Even John Calvin wrote to Melanchthon, objecting to it saying, "You extend adiaphora too far. Some of them plainly conflict with the Word of God. Now, since the Lord has drawn us into the fight, it behooves us to struggle all the more manfully" (Bente 101). Melanchthon desired to compromise already at Augsburg in 1530, but those who stood with him gave him the courage and strength to speak clearly and forcefully when it was needed. In this case, he perhaps thought that it was still possible to reach an understanding with the Roman Church so that the necessary reforms could take place. For him this was only an interim document leading to dialog and reform later.

Melanchthon and those who endorsed the Interim contributed to a long internal conflict among the Lutherans that would not be resolved until the Formula of Concord in 1577. The immediate conflict over the Interim forced those opposed to it to gather in Magdeburg, one Lutheran stronghold that still held out against the tide toward a return to the Roman Catholic Church. Even after Maurice captured Magdeburg, the opposition continued in other places. But the emperor's victory at Muhlberg was not the end of Luther's protest, no matter what Charles might have thought. As it had happened in the years after Worms, others protested boldly and strongly. They were convinced that the truths Luther proclaimed were more important than life and peace. In the final analysis, they considered those truths God's truths. ❦

1550

MAR 1552

Maurice opposes Charles V.

AUG 15, 1552

Treaty of Passau.

DEC 20, 1552

Katie Luther dies.

OCT 25, 1555

Charles announces abdication and plans to retire to monastery.

JAN 1558

Ferdinand, brother of Charles V, becomes emperor.

NOV 17, 1558

Elizabeth becomes queen of England.

1560

CHAPTER TWENTY

AUGSBURG, GERMANY

SEPTEMBER 25, 1555

Neither the Augsburg Interim nor the Leipzig Interim satisfied the Lutherans. They viewed their situation as nothing more than Spanish servitude. Maurice found himself in a difficult spot. He owed the emperor a great debt. The emperor had rewarded him the title of elector for his part in defeating the Smalcald League. But his own Saxons considered him a traitor. What they saw and felt was that he had denied the truth of God in order to obtain the electorate—a Judas. By contrast, John Frederick, deposed and now imprisoned by Charles, was considered a true Lutheran for his refusal to sign the Interim and his defiance of the emperor. All had not worked out as Maurice had thought. He felt betrayed by Charles because the emperor had promised humane treatment for his father-in-law, Philip of Hesse. Instead, Charles had imprisoned and humiliated Philip. John Frederick received the same treatment as Philip, but Maurice's feud with the former elector made his humiliation less important to him than the treatment of his father-in-law.

The Lutheran protest continued. While the Interim was put into effect in southern Germany, it was not carried out uniformly in the north. Yet the enforcement of the Augsburg Interim or the intended compromise of the Leipzig Interim left little room for doubt about how the religious question would be decided. Both documents leaned heavily to Roman Catholic teaching while the Council of Trent continued to trumpet the victory of Rome and the pope. In this situation neither the work of Melanchthon nor the current Wittenberg theologians offered even the smallest hope for the defeated Lutherans. The only exceptions were the Lutherans in Magdeburg, until they were driven to other places by Maurice.

The Council of Trent and the Protestants

In January 1547 the Sixth Session of the Council of Trent condemned the "erroneous doctrine of justification" (Schroeder 29). It said that justification "is not only a remission of sins *but also* the sanctification and renewal of the inward man through the voluntary reception of the grace and gifts whereby an unjust man *becomes* just" (Schroeder 33, emphasis added). The council defined faith as "the beginning of human salvation, the foundation and root of all justification" (35). The canons leave no doubt that Lutheran understanding falls under the condemnation of the Roman Catholic Church. Again and again Lutheran concepts are rejected and anyone who espouses them is condemned with "Let him be anathema (cursed)."

Later in 1547 the pope moved the council to Bologna, closer to Rome. That decision was not acceptable to Charles. He was interested in reforming the papacy and the church, but the pope insisted that the reforms should be left to the papacy. The Italian delegation moved to Bologna, but the rest stayed in Trent. After two years of tension and argument, Paul III suspended the Bologna assembly. Paul died at the age of 81 on November 10, 1549. Julius III, who succeeded Paul, reconvened the Council of Trent in May 1551. That session extended an invitation for the Protestants to come to Trent and address the assembly and provided safe-conduct. Charles also gave the German delegates safe-conduct. But the session took a clear turn toward Roman Catholic doctrine. It resolved that the priest changes the bread and wine into the body and blood of Christ when he consecrates the elements, affirming the Roman Catholic doctrine.

For some in Germany it appeared to be a waste of time to travel to Trent. But Charles insisted that they attend. So they came. Before leaving Germany, the Lutherans agreed to stand on the doctrine of the *Augsburg Confession* and Luther's Catechism. In addition, Melanchthon was commissioned to write an explanation of the Augsburg Confession, which was called the *Repetition of the Augsburg Confession* and later became known as the *Saxon Confession.*

It was different in tone from the *Augsburg Confession.* This confession did not step lightly; it was a refutation of Rome's assertions. In 1530 the Protestant princes hoped for a reunion with a reformed Rome. In 1547 that hope was gone. Melanchthon asserted that the unalterable basis of all teaching was only the Scriptures as they were understood by the ancient church and expressed in the ecumenical creeds—Apostles', Nicene, and Athanasian. Two articles of the Apostles' Creed became important in Melanchthon's defense of the *Augsburg Confession:* "the forgiveness of sins" and "one holy

Christian church." When Christians confess that they believe in "the forgiveness of sins," Melanchthon wrote that their confession excludes justification by works and earning satisfaction by a Christian's service to Christ. When they confess their faith in "one holy Christian church," they turn away from the political and secular concept of Rome and its assertion of superiority. Instead, they asserted that the church was a spiritual communion of believers in Christ. Other differences with Rome were also treated under articles following the order of the articles in the *Augsburg Confession.* The *Saxon Confession* was adopted by the northern Protestants in Wittenberg and signed by the theologians of Saxony on July 9.

A second confession was also prepared by the Protestant churches in the south called the *Wurttemberg Confession.* In its 35 articles it also restates the teachings of the *Augsburg Confession* and asserts that the teaching of the reformers agree with the doctrine of the apostles and of the early church. Their confession was sent on to Wittenberg. There both confessions were endorsed. The Lutherans agreed to send both confessions—the *Saxon Confession,* representing northern Germany (Saxony) and the *Wurttemberg Confession,* representing southern Germany.

The delegates traveled to Rome united in their protest. When they arrived, however, they did not receive a hearing before the whole Council of Trent. Instead, they addressed a private congregation. In that meeting they proposed that the decrees of the councils of Constance and Basel that asserted the superiority of councils over the popes should be confirmed, that previous decisions and decrees of the council be annulled, and that new discussions on the issues take place where Protestant theologians and leaders would be adequately represented. Julius III would not allow consideration of these proposals. The council instead postponed action on the Protestant proposals until March 19 when additional Protestant delegates could be present. The Protestants never returned.

Reversal

Melanchthon was also ordered to attend the Council of Trent in January 1552 and went to Nuremberg to await instructions. But he never went on to Trent. Events quickly changed. Maurice had turned against the emperor and joined the Lutheran protest against Charles in 1551. The following year, at the end of January, the Lutherans signed a pact with Henry II of France for financial support against the emperor. Henry was given the towns of Metz, Cambrai, Toul, and Verdun in exchange for his assistance. Charles was unprepared for their campaign. His forces were deployed in Italy. On the other hand, Maurice had kept an army in the field and moved against the emperor. Facing Maurice's forces at Innsbruck, Charles fled rather than become a prisoner. He moved to Villach with not much more than a bodyguard and sought refuge with his brother Ferdinand.

The changes in Germany were felt by those loyal to the Roman Catholic Church. Charles and Ferdinand squabbled over who was to become the next emperor after they were both gone—each one working to advance his own son. The Lutherans had seized the opportunity and negotiated with Ferdinand, limiting the help he might offer to his brother Charles. With Maurice's forces in the field, the Council of Trent was threatened by the reversal of their cause. No armed force was strong enough at this time to oppose Maurice and those allied against Charles. In April 1552, Julius III suspended the Council for two years because "such tumults and wars were enkindled by the craftiness of the enemy of the human race, that the council was at much inconvenience compelled to pause" (Schroeder 120). No new sessions of the council took place until Pius IV reconvened it in 1562.

The future of the Protestants, which looked so bleak in 1547, was now reversed. The Lutherans negotiated their demands with Charles and Ferdinand at Passau in Bavaria. They presented three demands: recognition of their liberties as Protestants, revocation of the Interim, and general amnesty for all rulers who fought against the emperor during the Muhlberg campaign. They also requested the release of Philip of Hesse from imperial custody. Charles refused the first two. He felt as strongly as the Lutherans about his faith and said his support for the Roman Catholic Church was not negotiable. The Treaty of Passau that went into effect on August 15, 1552, gave amnesty to the opponents of Charles, released Philip, but postponed the first two issues to another imperial diet.

Charles was not yet ready to quietly acquiesce to these events. He went on the offensive after the treaty was signed. Henry II, king of France, had seized Metz as part of his alliance with the Lutherans, while Maurice humbled Charles. While the negotiations at Passau continued, the army of Charles gathered around their emperor. With more than 60,000 men he marched toward Metz to retake the city from the French. Charles had gained an ally in Albert Alcibiades II and laid siege to Metz, against the advice of his military staff. The siege failed. The French defended the city well, the emperor's forces were not prepared for the campaign, and the winter weather was brutal. Charles withdrew in January 1553. It was the last campaign he would lead. The people of Metz taunted the retreating emperor with a banner that read "*Non Ultra Metas*" (No further than Metz). The banner mocked the motto Charles V adopted for his coat of arms when he became emperor, *"Plus Ultra"* (Yet Further).

Charles retreated to the Netherlands. Alcibiades continued to ravage the area in hopes of carving out his own territory. With the help of Ferdinand, Maurice defeated Albert in July 1553, but Maurice was wounded in the battle and died three days later. He had given the Lutherans defeat and victory. The victory over Charles humbled the emperor. He was defeated and understood that he had lost the ability to change what had happened in Europe. It would not be either Catholic or Protestant, although the struggle would resume and become the long and difficult war we know as the Thirty Years' War (1618–1648).

Katie's Death

While Luther still lived, he had advised Katie to sell the property and move to smaller quarters after he died, but she refused. She left Wittenberg at the outbreak of the Smalcald War and then returned, but she had few resources to support herself after the war. In 1552 an outbreak of the plague and a harvest failure forced her to leave Wittenberg again and travel to Torgau with two of her children—Paul and Margarethe.

As she approached the city, the horses drawing the wagon balked. Katie got down from the wagon to calm the horses but fell into a puddle and was seriously injured. She was carried into Torgau and cared for there. She did not recover. After three months in bed she died on December 20, 1552. She was buried at Saint Mary's Church in Torgau. On her deathbed she is reported to have said, "I will stick to Christ as a burr to cloth." Melanchthon in his obituary complained about the way she was treated after Luther's death. He noted that she had to wander around in great danger like an outlaw and also had to experience enormous ingratitude. She was deeply disappointed that those who could have helped her did not.

England

The reversal of the Protestant cause continued in England too. The death of Henry VIII in 1547 sent England into a period of uncertainty. He had turned from the Roman Catholic Church to secure a male heir for England. The son he so desperately wanted, Edward, became king of England at age 10. He died at 15, leaving the throne to Mary I. Her claim was disputed because of the fear that England would revert to the Roman Catholic Church under her rule; however, she did ascend to the throne as England's first ruling queen.

Charles V sent ambassadors to England to seek a marriage with Mary for his son Philip. The hope was to reclaim England for the Catholic Church and to bring it within the control of the empire. Because English law stated that the property and titles of a woman became her husband's upon marriage, this marriage with Philip had political implications for the family of Charles and religious implications in the tension between Protestants and Catholics. For a moment it looked as if England would return to the Roman Catholic Church. But parliament restricted Philip's future by limiting his title as king of England to Mary's lifetime.

Mary's reign did not last long. She began her reign after Edward died in 1553. Although she promised not to force anyone in England to accept her religion, Protestants were arrested and executed. She has become known as "Bloody Mary" because of her execution of Protestants. Mary died in 1558 without an heir, and Elizabeth became queen of England. Under her reign, England became more firmly Protestant. England's turn toward the Protestant side altered the history of the western world. Earlier uncontested Spanish exploration and colonization brought the Roman Catholic religion to much of the new world. The defeat of the Spanish Armada in 1588 became a significant religious event as well. Soon English exploration and colonization brought about the British Empire, and with it came the Protestant faith wherever the British flag flew. Those events, however, all lay in the future.

Charles Retires

In Europe, Charles had been emperor at a time of great turmoil. He had failed to defeat the Turks and had also failed to put an end to the Lutheran heresy and restore a united church. The Peace of Passau was a bitter medicine for him to swallow. When the Diet of Augsburg convened in 1555, it was clear that the Peace of Passau (1552) would be made permanent. Charles chose not to be present and turned the diet over to his brother Ferdinand. He did not wish to take responsibility for making Lutheranism legal in the empire.

The Peace of Augsburg recognized both Lutheran and Catholic faiths. Lutheran leaders were guaranteed equal security with Catholics. Each territory was given the right to choose between the two faiths . Church lands seized by Lutherans before Passau were to be retained. Catholics agreed to allow those who converted to leave their territories. This provision prevented Catholics from using the term *heretic* to impose penalties on Lutherans. But if a Catholic leader became Protestant, he would forfeit his title, lands, and privileges. The Lutherans objected to this, but it was included. The Peace permitted toleration in places where Catholics and Protestants lived together for years, including the city of Augsburg. While the idea of religious freedom was not yet completely acknowledged, Europe took a step in that direction. Unfortunately, religious conflict would continue, but for now peace prevailed.

Seeing the handwriting on the wall, Charles began to turn over his titles and power to his son Philip and his brother Ferdinand. He desired to be remembered as a ruler who had done his best but finally had failed to accomplish his most cherished goals—unity in one Christian church and victory over the Turks. His retirement was an unusual step for a ruling leader. He left Brussels for Spain on August 8, 1556, and spent the next years in Yuste, Spain, where he had built a residence next to a monastery. It was a modest villa richly decorated. He died there two years later on September 21, 1558. For salvation he depended on the intercession of his monks, his charity to the poor, and the Masses to be said for his soul. ❦

1550

Sep 25, 1555

Peace of Augsburg; Lutherans gain legal protection.

Sep 21, 1558

Charles dies.

May 28, 1577

Formula of Concord presented.

1588

English defeat of Spanish Armada.

1618–1648

Thirty Years' War.

1630

Gustavus Adolphus lands in Germany.

1648

Peace of Westphalia.

1650

CHAPTER TWENTY-ONE

POSTSCRIPT: FROM MONK TO BEGGAR

A young Catholic man about 22 years old made his way from home back to the university. He was studying law at Erfurt in Germany. The young man had already distinguished himself in his studies. His father was proud of his ambitious and intelligent son. In fact, he had purchased a set of law books for him as an encouragement and a tangible proof of his approval. The year was 1505 and the young student of law was Martin Luther.

For all his success, Martin was troubled by his relationship with God. As Martin returned to the university, he no doubt had questions about his standing before God. Was he righteous, or good enough, for God to accept him? How could he be a good person in God's eyes? In his mind and the mind of the church at the time, the righteousness of God was a standard every human had to meet. Catholic teaching said that God required people to be good or righteous before he would accept them. The life of service for God by a monk was a sure highway to God's approval. But he was not dedicating his entire life to God as the monks did. He wondered about these things. Perhaps he put the question in the framework of his future profession—a lawyer. How could he ever be good enough for God's standards? Was he able to do enough to win God's approval as a lawyer? How could he ever be as righteous and holy as the monks?

Whether Martin noticed the sky or not along the way, no one knows. But the weather began to change. He quickened his step as he heard the thunder rumble in the distance. It was moving quickly in his direction. Then the storm suddenly broke with surprising fury over his head. A flash of lightning and the crack of thunder were so near he thought he would die with the next flash and crack. In desperation and panic he prayed, "St. Anne, help me. I'll become a monk." Later, Luther remembered that this storm occurred near Stotternheim.

Perhaps the words of Martin Luther are not exactly accurate; they were, after all, spoken under duress in fear of impending danger. Yet the storm, with its flashes of lightning and cracks of thunder, changed his life. In the years ahead, the change created by this moment on the road would expand like the ripples after a stone thrown into a calm pool of water. In the days that followed, Luther wondered if his vow to become a monk came only from a spur-of-the-moment panic. He was not obliged to fulfill a vow spoken under duress. But finally, it didn't matter. He decided to fulfill his vow. He abandoned the law and entered the monastery in Erfurt.

Over 40 years later, Luther lay on his deathbed in the town where he was born. In order to get to Eisleben, he had braved the winter cold, flooding rivers, and ice flows. He was requested to go in order to settle a dispute. After he arrived, he succeeded in settling the dispute but then a painful tightness in the chest signaled the end. He died just a short distance from the house where he was born. The last words he wrote were on a slip of paper. The note included the words, "We are beggars, that is true" (Brecht, *Pres.* 375). It was a long journey for Luther to come from "St. Anne, help me. I'll become a monk" to "We are beggars." But the journey is the heart of the Reformation.

Becoming a Monk

In 1505, the lightning bolt on the road was a power over which he had no control. To Luther in the storm it must have represented God's wrath and the reminder of an angry God demanding righteousness from him. Luther understood that he did not possess what God demanded. So he become a monk and believed that would help him achieve the necessary righteousness to appease God. Luther entered the monastery looking for peace and hope. He sought it by fasting, vigils, prayers, confession, and diligent study. He offered God what was inside him and what he could perfect inside himself by his efforts. He wanted to be that good person and be rewarded with God's approval. That was the Roman Catholic Church's way to heaven. God started the grace and faith within and then it must be perfected to become acceptable righteousness. If one continues to do what is inside oneself, one may stand before God. As Luther would discover from personal experience, it was an impossible task.

As a faithful Catholic he believed that if his efforts as a monk were not enough, the church promised that he had a millennia of time in purgatory to suffer in order to be purged of sin and the pollution of the flesh. In addition, his own prayers, the prayers of others, the excess good works of the special saints, and Masses said on his behalf could reduce the time in purgatory. When he was sent to Rome in 1510, he eagerly went hoping to do all he could to earn what still seemed so elusive. He also lamented his inability to help his parents. He wanted to help them out of purgatory by his pilgrimage, Masses, and prayers in the holy city, but he could not because they were still living back in Germany.

As a monk, he was diligent in his efforts, sincere, devoted, and rigidly regular—even overzealous—in confession of his sins. He attempted to confess every single one of his sins so he could obtain absolution. Luther said later that if anyone could obtain salvation as a monk, he would be one of them. But he was troubled by all the effort. He found no peace. Hope seemed to slip away instead of growing as he punished himself with fasting and work. What was inside of him was not good enough no matter how diligent the effort. He did not have enough to offer God in exchange for his love and acceptance. His troubles led him to his superior, John Staupitz. After listening to Luther's questions and turmoil, Staupitz advised him to look to the cross of Christ for comfort.

The advice of his superior helped, but in those early days, Luther was still confused. Staupitz sent him to Wittenberg to teach at the new university established by Elector Frederick the Wise. There he read, taught, and thought. He lectured on the Psalms and eventually on Romans. The study of Romans was a turning point like the storm of Stotternheim. His study of Paul's letter turned his thinking away from the angry God of the thunderbolt demanding righteousness. Instead, God mercifully opened his eyes to something much different than he had taught and believed.

A New Insight

For his Romans class, Luther customarily entered the lecture hall Monday and Friday morning at 6:00 A.M. to dictate his notes and comments to his students. In his preparation for his classes, he was troubled by Paul's words on "the righteousness of God" in Romans 1:17: "In the gospel the righteousness from God is revealed—a righteousness that is by faith from first to last." He thought day and night about the passage and its meaning. Up to this point, he considered righteousness something he gave to God. But as he struggled to find the meaning of Paul's words, he began to understand the "righteousness of God" as the righteousness God gives sinners through faith in Jesus Christ. It was not a standard sinners had to match by their efforts. Contrary to all his efforts as a monk, righteousness was not something that came from inside him but something different that God gave—a righteousness that is alien to what was inside and came from God for the sake of Christ. He had realized how imperfect his own efforts at becoming righteous were. Now he found that Christ's righteousness given by God himself was perfect and complete.

Later he said that this revelation made him feel like he had been born again and the gates of heaven were suddenly open. He was transformed from a monk working for a reward from God to a beggar receiving God's boundless and wonderful gifts. As a humble beggar, God gave it to him along with every other gift. What he needed to be a good person in God's eyes came as a gift from God himself—by grace—and he possessed it by trust—by faith—in God's promise in Christ.

He had been following the teaching and tradition of the church, but he had found something completely different. He says he scanned the Scriptures from memory, looking for confirmation, and found it in many places. Then he confesses, "And now, where I had once hated the phrase 'the righteousness of God' so much, I began to love and extoll it as the sweetest of words so that this passage in Paul became the very gate of paradise for me. Afterwards, I read Augustine, *On the Spirit and the Letter,* where I found that he too, beyond my expectation, interpreted 'the righteousness of God' in the same way—as that which God bestows upon us, when he justifies us" (McGrath, 97). He grew confident of this gift because God said it was true. This new insight came from Paul's letter to the Romans—the Scriptures—not from his study of the decrees and pronouncements of the Roman Church.

Luther's Protest

Then came Tetzel and the indulgences. Their sale challenged his new thinking. Could Christians offer a gift—even to the church for a great cause such as the building of St. Peter's—in order to remove the church's requirement for satisfaction for sin. Could such an offering make Christians good? Taking money from ordinary Germans to build a church in Rome was one problem, but not as great as the implication that buying indulgences could release souls from purgatory and pave their entrance into heaven. Luther objected. His *95 Theses* challenged the abuse he saw in Germany. He wanted to discuss and debate whether the church had indeed adopted such a practice that accepted money with the promise that it would make the people better and help them escape what their sins deserved.

The resistance from Rome came quickly. Luther was summoned before Cardinal Cajetan in Augsburg to withdraw his objections. Cajetan, one of the leading theologians of his day, was told not to debate with Luther but to simply demand his retraction. The Roman cardinal pointed out the decrees and pronouncements of the popes that supported the teaching on indulgences. But when Luther left that interview, he realized that the revered cardinal had no scriptural proof for the practice. Even the questions Luther had raised on indulgences were not clearly settled by the Roman Catholic Church. Luther left frustrated. That clarification on indulgences appeared after Luther left Augsburg. Leo X issued a new decree clarifying indulgences that was based on Cajetan's report and advice (Schwiebert 356).

Luther moved on, unconvinced and undaunted. Luther's understanding of the gift of God through faith in Christ provided the courage to write and object even more vehemently. When summoned to Worms to retract his views, he stood boldly and confessed he would not change his views unless he could be convinced by the Scriptures. Righteousness was a gift from God, not an offering to him by sinners. He would not be moved from that great, comforting truth.

Many of the practices of the Roman Catholic Church were designed to help people become righteous by their devotion. Life as a monk, pilgrimages, indulgences, and the Mass itself all emphasized the sinner's need to have something to offer God. Luther opposed them all because he had been convinced that God alone could give sinners what they needed to be good, holy, and acceptable—Christ's righteousness by faith. Sinners are justified—declared righteous—by God as a gift of grace for Christ's sake through faith.

That important truth motivated Luther and guided his thoughts for the rest of his life. Luther may have stood alone at Worms, but he did not remain alone. Many read his words, reread their Bibles, and agreed. They also were ready to stand before the powers of the church and state as he did at Worms. They did so at Augsburg. However, that was not the end of their confession. Near the end of his life, Luther was asked to help them make another if they were called to confess at the council the pope convened at Trent. Elector John Frederick asked him to write a confession that would help guide them. Luther wrote the *Smalcald Articles*. That confession clearly identified how important the righteousness God gave sinners through Christ was:

> We hold that one is justified by faith apart from works of the law (Romans 3:28) that He might be just and the justifier of the one who has faith in Jesus (Romans 3:26). Nothing of this article can be yielded or surrendered, even though heaven and earth and everything else falls (Mark 13:31). For there is no other name under heaven given among

> men by which we must be saved (Acts 4:12), and with his stripes we are healed (Isaiah 53:5). Upon this article everything that we teach and practice depends, in opposition to the pope, the devil, and the whole world. Therefore, we must be certain and not doubt this doctrine. Otherwise, all is lost, and the pope, the devil, and all adversaries win the victory and the right over us. (SA Chief Article 4,5)

Luther even used the word *thunderbolt* in the *Smalcald Articles*—perhaps it is only a coincidence. When speaking of repentance, he identified the law of God as the thunderbolt that "strikes down both obvious sinners and false saints. He declares no one to be in the right, but drives them all together to terror and despair" (SA Repentance 2). But then, "To this office of the Law, the New Testament immediately adds the consoling promise of grace through the Gospel. This must be believed. As Christ declares, 'Repent and believe in the gospel' " (Mark 1:15). Law and gospel work together. The law comes so that all "can know what they are before God and acknowledge that they are lost." The gospel comes to "bring consolation and forgiveness" (SA Repentance 4,5,8). The gospel gives grace so that sinners—humbled like beggars before God by the law—can receive grace and accept from God the forgiveness of sins.

When Luther wrote that final note before he died—"We are beggars, that is true!"—he understood how unworthy he was before God. He had nothing in himself that could move God to love him. His life of service was not enough. Yet, in spite of that, God loved him simply because God loves sinful beggars. This God extends forgiveness, life, and salvation—righteousness—to undeserving sinners—a righteousness that does not come from inside any human, but comes from outside, from Christ. It is alien to human effort and human capabilities. It comes only from God through faith in Christ. ❦

We are beggars, that is true!

FOR FURTHER READING

Arand, Charles P., Robert Kolb, James A. Nestingen. *The Lutheran Confessions: History and Theology of The Book of Concord.* Minneapolis: Fortress Press, 2012.

Bainton, Roland H. *Here I Stand: A Life of Martin Luther.* Nashville: Abingdon Press, 1950.

Bente, Gerhard Friedrich. *Historical Introductions to the Lutheran Confessions.* St. Louis: Concordia Publishing House, 2005.

Blockmans, Wim. *Emperor Charles V 1500-1558.* Translated by Isola van den Hoven-Vaardon. New York: Arnold Publishers, 2002.

Bornkamm, Heinrich. *Luther in Mid-Career 1521-1530.* Philadelphia: Fortress Press, 1983.

Brandi, Karl. *The Emperor Charles V: The Growth and Destiny of a Man and of a World-Empire.* Translated by C. B. Wedgwood. Norwich, UK: Fleatcher & Son Ltd., 1939.

Brecht, Martin. *Martin Luther: His Road to Reformation 1483-1521.* Minneapolis: Fortress Press, 1985.

——— *Martin Luther: Shaping and Defining the Reformation 1521-1532.* Minneapolis: Fortress Press, 1990.

——— *Martin Luther: The Preservation of the Church 1532-1546.* Minneapolis: Fortress Press, 1990.

Concordia Triglotta: The Symbolical Books of the Ev. Lutheran Church. St. Louis: Concordia Publishing House, 1921.

D'Aubingne, J. H. Merle. *The Life and Times of Martin Luther: Selections.* Translated by H. White. Chicago: Moody Press, 1978.

Durant, Will. *The Reformation: A History of European Civilization from Wyclif to Calvin: 1300-1564.* New York: Simon and Schuster, 1957.

Graebner, August L. *Dr. Martin Luther: 1483-1546.* Trans. W. O. Loescher. New Ulm, MN: Graphic Arts Department, Martin Luther College, 2014.

Grimm, Harold J. *The Reformation Era: 1500-1650.* New York: The Macmillan Company, 1965.

Kittelson, James M. *Luther, the Reformer: The Story of the Man and His Career.* Minneapolis: Augsburg Publishing House, 1986.

Kleinschmidt, Harald. *Charles V: The World Emperor.* Phoenix Mill, UK: Sutton Publishing Limited, 2004.

Kolb, Robert and Charles P. Arand. *The Genius of Luther's Theology: A Wittenberg Way of Thinking for the Contemporary Church.* Grand Rapids: Baker Academic, 2008.

Kolb, Robert. *Martin Luther: Confessor of the Faith.* New York: Oxford University Press, 2009.

Kooiman, Willem. *Luther and the Bible.* Translated by John Schmidt. Philadelphia: Muhlenberg Press, 1961.

Luther, Martin. *Martin Luther's Basic Theological Writings.* Edited by Timothy F. Lull. Minneapolis: Fortress Press, 1989.

——— *Luther's Works.* Edited by Jaroslav Pelikan and Helmut T. Lehmann. American Edition. 55 vols. St. Louis: Concordia Publishing House; Philadelphia: Fortress Press, 1955–1986.

Maltby, William. *The Reign of Charles V.* New York: Palgrave, 2002.

McGrath, Alister. *Luther's Theology of the Cross.* Oxford: Blackwell Publishers Ltd., 1985.

Melanchthon, Philip. *The Loci Commines of Philip Melanchthon.* Translated by Charles Hill. Boston: Meador Publishing Company, 1944.

Oberman, Heiko A. *Luther: Man between God and the Devil.* Translated by Eileen Walliser-Schwarzbart. New Haven: Yale University Press, 1989.

Reu, M. *Luther's German Bible.* Columbus: Lutheran Book Concern, 1934.

Robinson, Paul W. *Martin Luther: A Life Reformed.* Saddle River, New Jersey: Longman, 2010.

Schroeder, H. J. *Cannons and Decrees of the Council of Trent: Original Text with English Translation.* St. Louis: B. Herder Book Company, 1941.

Schaff, Philip. *History of the Christian Church.* 8 vols. Grand Rapids, Michigan: Wm. B. Eerdmans Publishing Company, 1910.

Schwiebert, E. G. *Luther and his Times: The Reformation from a New Perspective.* St. Louis: Concordia Publishing House, 1950.

Wellman, Sam. *Frederick the Wise: Seen and Unseen Lives of Martin Luther's Protector.* St. Louis: Concordia Publishing House, 2015.

SUBJECT INDEX